COLD BLOODED KILLERS

By RJ Parker

COLD BLOODED KILLERS

By RJ Parker

Copyright © 2014

RJ Parker Publishing, Inc.

ISBN-13: 978-1500899257

ISBN-10: 1500899259

United States of America

6x9

Table of Contents

RJ PARKER

Acknowledgements

I thank my daughters Amanda and Katie who encourages me everyday. Without them, I may have given up to my disability and the chronic pain that goes with it. For those who have AS or any arthritic problem especially in their spine and hips, they know what I'm talking about. This book is for my daughter's mom, Ann Marie.

To my many fans and friends on FaceBook, thank you.

My grandson Parker Joseph was born on October 17, 2012 and he is my pride and joy.

Preface

The term Patricide refers to a child killing their father. The term Matricide refers to a child killing their mother and the term Parricide references a child killing both of his or her parents.

What type of child is capable of such an act of violence against a parent and under what circumstances could this happen? The literature suggests that these are neglected and abused children, more commonly, teenagers, who feel trapped with few options. They have had enough and they feel there is no other way out. Children cannot simply leave a bad situation as the law does not allow youths to run away and if caught, they will be returned to their legal guardian. Some do run away successfully but then find it difficult to survive on the streets with limited resources, limited skills, and insufficient money.

In many instances, parents grow dependent on the adolescence and the child has too many responsibilities looking after the household and their parents. Children going through adolescence need the support of their parents as it is an altering time in their lives.

The children who commit parricide are either the harshly abused child who is pushed beyond his or her limits, or the ruthlessly, mentally ill child or the severely rebellious child.

The abused child is the most commonly encountered kind of killer. They killed because they could no longer contend with their surroundings at home. These children were severely abused by one or both parents and repeatedly suffered sexual, physical, and verbal mistreatment as well. Classically, they do not have histories of severe mental illness or grave and extensive antisocial behavior. They are not criminally stylish. However, for them, the killings symbolize an act of desperation.

The ruthless mentally ill child can kill on occasion. These children have lost contact with reality and their medical records will indicate that prior psychiatric treatments have failed. In most cases, they are deemed unfit to stand trial due to insanity.

There have been few children who have killed without remorse and yet their parents were kind and loving. This dangerously antisocial child is frequently the silage of news captions. These young offenders characteristically display improper conduct and severe disorderly behavior that continues for several months.

These are the children that kill their parents solely for some kind of self-seeking reasons.

Few severely abused children actually kill

their parents. But most are at a high risk of becoming negligent or socially dependent rather than children who are treated well by concerned parents or loving guardians. Most often, the damage relinquished because of child abuse does not manifest itself until a generation later.

The undeniable realities and effects of child abuse are increasingly being recognized as the responsibility of everyone in the culture. Yet society has failed these children. It has failed to make a sufficient commitment to all children. It has clearly failed to protect these children and it has failed to foster good parenting.

Parenting skills and parental support are areas that desperately need attention. Education needs to be made available to help parents cope with the stresses of raising children, particularly young parents or parents of children with special needs. Research shows that increasing the knowledge of parents about home and child management, and enhancing the development of good communication skills, healthy emotional ties, and parent-child bonding helps prevent child abuse.

Chapter 1: Bryan and David Freeman

Dennis and Brenda Freeman

Discovery of the bodies

On February 27, 1995 the Police discovered the bludgeoned bodies of Dennis Freeman, 54, his wife Brenda, 48 and their son Eric, 11 in their Salisbury, PA home. The immediate suspects were the older children, Bryan, 17, and David, 16, who had shaved and tattooed their heads as a symbol of their Neo-Nazi beliefs.

Dennis Freeman was a High School Custodian and Brenda a Homemaker. They were devout Jehovah Witnesses and raised their children according to the strict rules of their beliefs, which included: no birthday celebrations, no voting, no participation in any form of military, and no recognition of national holidays. The older boys resented it deeply. When Bryan took an interest in joining the military, his parents first noticed the trouble with their son and his anger issues. They tried various programs in dealing with Bryan's anger, but several times he threatened to kill them.

On February 27, 1995 his threats would become reality. Early that afternoon Brenda's sister Valerie arrived at the family home to find the front and back doors locked, and also the garage door. However since Dennis's truck was in the driveway she assumed he was home. She found the sliding door on the side of the house unlocked so she entered but found the house to be cool and unusually quiet. She slowly walked to Erik's closed bedroom door. It was then that she knew something was wrong and a feeling of dread came over her. She hesitantly opened Erik's door and was faced with her nephew's blood-splattered body. She silently bit back a scream and proceeded to the master bedroom where she came upon another body lying on a blood-soaked bed.

Erik Freeman, age 11

Valerie ran from the house to a neighbor's

and phoned the police. Officer Michael Pochran responded first at the scene but before entering the house he called for backup. The first thing the police discovered upon entering the house was a bloody aluminum baseball bat, leaning against the dining room cabinet. In the master bedroom they found Dennis, beaten to death: his face and head were smashed in and his brains were exposed and his neck was slashed. The second victim, 11 year old Erik was on his bed, bloody and bashed. Apparently they hated their young brother Erik just as much as their parents because he didn't resist their parent's teachings.

They searched each room but couldn't find Brenda, until they proceeded to the basement. On one of the steps they found a bloody metal pipe. They found Brenda lying on her side with her nightgown pulled up and a knife at her side. She had been stabbed repeatedly. On a wall above the body, two swastikas had been drawn.

As the house began to fill with Police Officers and Homicide Detectives, it was clear that Bryan and David were missing and so was the family car. Given their reputation as white supremacists and their history of aggression, the hunt was on to find these boys and their cousin Nelson Birdwell III, whom they were known to associate with.

Background on the killers

David Freeman, age 16

David was 6' 3" and weighed 245 pounds. He had tattooed Sieg Heil on his forehead and Bryan had Berzerker on his. Their classmates, teachers and friends confirmed that they were impressive and threatening but students also said they were well respected. In 1992, David was in and out of various rehabilitation centers for substance abuse. He was eventually committed to a hospital where he stayed for one month. The doctors evaluated him and determined him to be of above-average intelligence but with an antisocial personality disorder.

Bryan Freeman, age 17

Bryan was 6' and 215 pounds at the time of his arrest. He was known to be more polite and intelligent than his brother and even made the honor roll in school. But, he too experimented with drugs and was in and out of treatment centers. It was in one of these centers where another boy encouraged him to join the skinheads.

Skinheads are a despotic youth movement which sanctifies violence as a means to attain political domination. Their objectives are a clutter of slogans including defending the white race and building white pride. They are open in their expressions of anti-Jewish, anti-black, anti-gay, anti-Hispanic, anti-Asian, and anti-immigrants. Their name originally came from their shaved heads, although currently most let their hair grow to lessen their visibility. Tattoos are also part of Skinhead appearance and members decorate their bodies with tattoos of white power slogans and symbols such as swastikas. Nazi regalia such as the Iron Cross and the SS badge are also part of their distinctive clothing.

So upon his return home, Bryan encouraged David to get involved in the skinheads and after attending several meetings they decided to form their own group with their cousin Benny Birdwell. Early in the investigation, Police were able to learn from schoolmates about Bryan's and David's association with Skinheads and that they bragged about decapitating a cat and worshipping its body.

Nelson (Benny) Birdwell III, age 18

The three boys shaved their heads, got tattoos and proclaimed their loyalty to the white supremacist movement. Bryan was enraged that his parents continued to place him in treatment facilities as he viewed these places as 'mental institutes'. David soon adopted the same behavior and attitude toward his parents. Both would terrorize their brother Erik who they considered a wimp and a momma's boy. They also terrified the parents. The parents tried tough-love by taking things from their sons. This enraged them even more. Brenda sold her sons cars...the boys in turn tattooed their heads. Brenda and Dennis stripped all paraphernalia pertaining to hate from their sons rooms. It was during the removal of Nazi posters and pamphlets they discovered a book about killing ones parents. This was just three weeks before they were killed. On February 23, two days prior to the killing, they were overheard saying that they were going to kill their mother. David was also suspended from school for getting into an altercation which erupted into threats of violence against the principal.

Apprehension

After interviewing Harry Liste, a classmate, the Police learned that the brothers had mentioned killing their parents and heading to Florida but the trio in fact went west to Michigan. A truck driver heard about the murders and the descriptions of the three boys and called authorities indicating they were at the Truck World Motor Inn in Hubbard, Ohio. A videotape from a nearby grocery store also captured the boy's picture. This video was sent back to the Allentown police department where the suspects were positively identified by outraged family members.

Unfortunately, by the time police arrived, they were long gone. But, they had made phone calls from the Inn to Frank Hesse, another skinhead, in Hope, Michigan. The day they arrived in Michigan, some six hundred miles from home, they decided to go ice fishing with their friend. While they were gone, S.W.A.T. Members from the Michigan State Police along with assistance from the FBI surrounded the house. Upon their return at 6:00 pm from fishing, they were apprehended.

David's Story

David and Bryan Freeman had previously decided that if they were caught, they would take the fall instead of their cousin Benny. They assumed that they would be tried as juveniles, and Benny would be tried as an adult. So David waived his right to a lawyer and offered up a statement.

According to David the evening before the bodies were discovered, all three of the boys went to the movies where they saw 'Murder in the First' and then returned home at 10:30pm. He said that both Dennis and Erik were asleep however Brenda had waited up for them. They climbed through the basement window and were in the process of calling some friends to go drinking when their mother heard them. She came downstairs to tell the boys to go to bed and Benny to go home. Benny obeyed but never went home. It's reported that Brenda came down three times and asked Benny to leave and each time he would crawl out the window but return. The third time is when the murders took place. David said that Brenda and Bryan were yelling at each other and that he really never witnessed what actually happened. He did implicate his brother Bryan in the killing of his mother. He said that Bryan threatened to stab both him and Benny and then ordered them to go upstairs and get their father and brother. David admitted to killing his father Dennis and brother Erik and said that Benny just watched, following from one room to the other, but never participating in the murders. They placed the baseball bat in the dining room and the knives in the kitchen sink, changed their clothes and left the house. While the detectives listened to David's story, Benny was telling other investigators a whole different story.

Benny's Story

Benny's parents arrived to be with him in Michigan after he was arrested. They were very distraught as Benny was not a troublesome child and appeared to be an all-around nice kid. Benny reiterated about going to Wendy's, then the movies and then returning home. He also confirmed that Brenda came downstairs repeatedly and asked him to go home and that he pretended to leave and came back each time. When questioned about the murders, he said that Bryan and Brenda were screaming at each other and Bryan stabbed Brenda in the back as she was leaving to go upstairs. She pulled the knife out of her back and attacked Bryan. They fought over the knife and Bryan eventually stabbed her in the shoulder. When she screamed this time, Bryan forced a pair of shorts into her mouth so that she wouldn't wake Dennis. After a few minutes she laid still.

He said that Bryan and Dennis went upstairs to kill Dennis and Erik and that he remained in the basement. He was called upstairs after the other two killings and saw that Bryan was covered in blood and went to change his clothes. David didn't look bloody but went out to the backyard and vomited. They took all the cash, about $200 out of Dennis's wallet, argued in the car about where to go and eventually deciding on going to a friend's farm in Michigan. They contemplated going back and staging the scene to look like a robbery gone bad but heard the news on the radio so it was already too late.

Bryan's Story

Bryan and David read an article in the Midland News and felt that Benny was putting all the blame on them so they decided to retaliate. Before Bryan gave a statement for the first time, he requested certain conditions: he wanted a lawyer for him and his brother, he wanted the death penalty taken off the table and they wanted to give an interview to a reporter of their choosing. The deal was approved by the prosecution.

Bryan told a similar story but with more details and admitting his own involvement in the murders. He confessed that after he killed his mother, Benny used the handle of a pick ax to bludgeon her over the head, and then went upstairs to help David. Bryan did deny telling the others to go and kill Dennis and Erik. Bryan started to cry while giving his statement and said that Ben told him how he shattered Erik's skull and hit both Erik and Dennis in the face several times with a baseball bat. He admitted that Ben had cut their throats and that they were going to take the fall for Benny.

The Arraignment

The three boys were extradited back to Allentown and taken to the Lehigh County Jail where they were each officially charged. The arraignment for the brothers was on April 26. The Coroner was first to be called and his testimony confirmed the following.

Dennis had been killed first, struck six times on the head, seven times on the chest which fractured the breastbone and ribs. He had fractures on the neck, eye sockets, nose and jaw. The brain had actually protruded through the skull. He had been struck with two different weapons indicating there were two different attackers. The cause of death was extreme brain trauma. Brenda was the next to die and her death was caused by multiple stab wounds. She was stabbed through the heart and lung plus the right scapula and a shoulder stabbing that was 5 inches deep. Erik died from excessive head injuries. He was beaten on his head, face, torso and arms. The fractures and bruises on his arms indicated that he tried to defend himself from the aluminum bat.

The prosecution again announced that if the boys admitted to first-degree murder they would receive life in prison and not the death penalty. Both declined as their lawyers again thought they would be tried as juveniles. But as time went by, it was evident that if the lawyers continued to press for a juvenile trial, they would likely lose and then their strategy would be revealed to the prosecution.

So on December 7, Bryan ended the possibility of a trial by admitting to killing his mother. A week later, David also admitted his guilt and told the judge that he had taken part in the killing of his father and brother. Both were sentenced to life in prison. Nelson "Benny" Birdwell was only convicted of first-degree murder in the death of Dennis Freeman and was sentenced to life in prison without parole.

Chapter 2: Edmund Kemper

AKA The Co-ed Killer

Edmund "Big Ed" Kemper III stands 6' 9" and weighs in at over 300 pounds and was an active serial killer in the early 1970's in California. At the age of 15 years old, he murdered his grandparents. He would later go on to kill six female hitchhikers as well as his mother and her friend. At an early age, Kemper exhibited sociopathic behavior including playing with his sister's dolls, stabbing cats, and weird sexual rituals. His mother was an alcoholic and would verbally abuse him. She would also make him sleep in the basement in fear that he would rape his little sister. Unlike his mother, Edmund had a close relationship with his father so when they divorced he was devastated and blamed his mother.

In 1963, Edmund, 15, ran away from home and searched for his father in Van Nuys only to find out that his father had remarried and had another son. His father sent him back to his mother who in turn sent him to live with his grandparents, Edmund and Maude Kemper, in Montana. Considering the rejections from his parents it is not surprising that he never had a good relationship with them.

On August 27, 1964, Edmund and his grandmother got into an argument and he fatally shot her in the head. Then he stabbed her repeatedly. He waited until his grandfather returned from the grocery store and also killed him with a gun. Edmund called his mother and she encouraged him to call the police and turn himself in, which he did.

He was committed to a state hospital where he stayed for almost five years before being released to his mother's care. He later convinced psychologists that he was mentally recovered and thus had his juvenile records sealed. In 1972, Kemper started his serial killings.

Kemper was driving in Berkeley on May 7, 1972 when he picked up hitchhikers Mary Ann Pesce and Anita Luchessa, students from Fresno State. He drove to a secluded wooded area near Alameda where he smothered Pesce and then stabbed both her and Anita to death. He carried their corpses to his apartment in the trunk of his car. In the apartment, he dismembered both bodies, took pictures of the body parts and even had oral sex with Mary Ann's decapitated head. He then disposed of the body parts in a ravine.

September 14, 1972, Aiko Koo, 15, was waiting for a bus when she decided to hitchhike instead. Kemper drove up, pointed a gun at her to get in the car and then proceeded to strangle her. This time he took her body back to his mother's house where he raped and dissected her body. After dismembering Aiko, he buried the head in his mother's flower garden as a joke. He later said that his mother 'always wanted people looking up to her'. The remaining body parts were buried in his mother's backyard.

Kemper was driving around Cabrillo College Campus on the night of January 7, 1973 when he picked up Cindy Schall, 19, and drove her to a wooded area where he killed her with a .22 caliber handgun. Again, he brought the body home in his trunk to his mother's house where he had sex with the body before dissecting it in the bathtub. He removed the bullet from the girls head and buried the decapitated head in the garden. The remaining body parts were discarded in a ravine.

On February 5, 1973, Edmund went hunting for victims after having a heated discussion with his mother. He encountered Rosalind Thorpe, 24, and Allison Liu, 23, at the UC Santa Cruz Campus. After getting in his car, Kemper shot and killed both girls with his .22 handgun. After wrapping the bodies in a blanket, he drove to his mother's house again where he dismembered them while his mother was in the backyard tending to her garden. He had sex with their bodies and discarded them off a cliff.

On April 20, 1973 (Good Friday), Kemper killed his mother with a hammer while she slept. He then cut off her head which he first used for oral sex before using it as a dart board. He put her vocal chords in the garbage disposal because he said 'she bitched and screamed at me for years'. He then invited his mother's friend Sally Hallett, 59, to come over to the house. Upon her arrival he strangled her to death and left the crime scene as it was, without cleaning anything up.

Kemper left California and while driving through Colorado he heard about the murder of his mother and her friend on the radio. He called the police and confessed then he waited for a patrol car to come and arrest him.

He pleaded not guilty by reason of insanity, however, in November 1973 he was convicted of eight counts of murder.

Chapter 3: Stephen Arnold Ford

Steve, 38, and his wife Kathleen, 37 had two children, Stephen 17 and Jennifer 15. They were a normal, average family. They lived on a quiet street in Airdrie, Alberta, Canada.

Despite normal everyday family issues, their only big concern was Stephen. When he was 9 years old, he was assaulted by a babysitter and was quite traumatized. He received several years of treatment and counseling but to no avail. At age 10, he tried to commit suicide by slashing his wrists.

Stephen became a rebellious teen. He would stay out late at night, sometimes using alcohol or drugs. He turned to petty crime, then to breaking and entering and finally armed robbery. He was out of control at 16. The tension mounted in the house, and the neighbours reported constant nightly screaming and fighting. Kathleen became depressed and began suffering from nightmares and migraines. Her doctor prescribed Valium to help calm her anxiety as well as anti-depressants. Steve was also stressed to the point he had developed heart problems and palpitations.

At age17, Stephen attempted suicide again when he swallowed 62 of his mother's anti-depressants pills. A friend found Stephen and his suicide note and called an ambulance. He was revived but the doctors doubted his chances of a full recovery and thought he might remain in a coma or die. But, a week later he did recover fully and underwent extensive psychiatric treatment. Prior to being released from hospital, Steve and Kathleen sought additional advice from counselors and they attempted to instigate rules in the house. They sold their home and moved to Calgary hoping to start a new life, a new beginning for the family of four. But it seemed that his parents were afraid to enforce the rules in fear that he would retaliate or try to commit suicide again. Tough-love also didn't seem to work. Stephen quit school, started committing criminal acts again, and was diagnosed with an anti-social disorder.

On August 1, 1989, Stephen's sister, Jennifer was babysitting overnight for her cousin. Her dad was to pick her up at 9:30am the next morning.

This same evening Stephen and a few friends watched "Bat 21" a violent Vietnam war movie on TV, while his parents slept upstairs. Stephen was drunk and in the mood to party. According to Stephen, their dog urinated on his foot and at that point, he lost control and became violent. He went out to the shed, picked up an axe and proceeded to his parent's bedroom where he hacked his father to death with twenty-two blows. His mother woke in a panic, screaming. He silenced her as well by chopping her with the axe twenty times.

Stephen then stole his parents cash, credit cards and vehicle and headed to Swift Current, Saskatchewan, where he stopped at a mall and using his father's Visa card, went on a shopping spree. Arriving in Moose Jaw he took a small room at the Park Lodge Motel and called the RCMP in Airdie to report his crime. He confessed to killing his parents. He told the officer, "I don't want to be hurt. I just want to be treated good."

Prior to this, Jennifer was at her cousins waiting for her father to pick her up. Calling the house and receiving no answer, she knew something was terribly wrong. She called a cab and went home, only to find both her parents lying on their bed with blood everywhere. Had she not been babysitting, she too may have been a murder victim.

Stephen was found guilty on two counts of second-degree murder and was sentenced to life with no chance of parole for twenty years. On August 1, 2009, exactly twenty years after killing his parents, Stephen was granted a full parole and walked out of prison.

Chapter 4: Michael Alborgeden

Michael's parents, Craig and Peggy Alborgeden began dating in Junior High School but Craig was an abusive boyfriend. Peggy always wore heavy makeup to conceal the bruises and would avoid taking physical education so that she wouldn't have to shower with her classmates and then have to explain the marks. She had hoped that Craig would change and stop abusing her. But that never happened and the abuse only escalated. Typical of any abuser, he would warn her that if she told anyone he would kill her. He'd apologize and make vague promises not to hit her again, but it never lasted.

By the time Peggy entered Senior High, she was pregnant with Michael. She believed that by giving Craig a child, he would change and he did for a short time. During her ninth month of pregnancy Craig punched her in the stomach which caused her water to break. This complicated the delivery, however, both baby and mother survived. When Peggy turned twenty-one she decided she had enough of Craig's beatings. She called her mother to tell her she was coming home. However, Craig overheard the conversation. Just after she hung up the telephone, he punched her in the face twice and made Peggy call her mother back to tell her she had changed her mind and would be staying with Craig.

When he finally allowed her to see a doctor three days later, she was immediately hospitalized. He had broken her jaw so bad that it had to be wired shut for two months. This was her first trip to the hospital but certainly wouldn't be her last.

During the next twelve years she would be treated for concussions, broken bones, and cuts. Michael first learned to conceal the truth about Craig's abusive behavior from his mother. Michael did not escape his father's violence either. He also was abused. However, Craig never hit Michael in front of his wife. He was afraid she would take action and report him to the police or child services.

Peggy and Craig's marriage finally ended in divorce. Initially Michael lived with his mother. But just four months after his parents divorce, Michael was arrested and put on probation for breaking into a neighbour's house. His mother then decided it would be best for Michael to leave the area and go live with his father, Craig. He and his father had some good times, and Craig spoiled his son with cars, dirt bikes, fishing and hunting trips. Michael also worked part-time at the service station with his father. All of these great times didn't last long. Soon Craig had changed again and started abusing Michael. Craig called his special punishments GP's, short for 'general purpose'. These were the punishments Michael would receive every day regardless of his father's mood.

Michael described a GP as a hit for no reason. His father would walk by him and just hit him with a closed fist on the chest, arms or legs. The other hits were inflicted when Craig was angry. Michael also learned to accept death threats as part of his life.

From the age of 10, Michael no longer cried when his father abused him. Craig wanted his son to "take the punishment like a man." If he did cry after a beating, he would be hit again. Michael learned to block out his feelings and deny the pain. The idea of discussing his abuse with anyone was simply out of the question. Not only was he very embarrassed about the situation, but his father constantly reminded him it would be bad for his health to complain to anyone. In short, his father said that he would kill him if he told anyone, including his mother.

A friend, Kenny Stuggans, witnessed Craig abuse Michael countless times. One time he tried to stick up for Michael but Craig punched Kenny in the stomach and said, "Keep your fuckin' mouth shut or you're not going to walk away." Kenny never attempted to interfere again.

At age14, Michael had a girlfriend named Jennifer. Soon she began to understand Michael's relationship with his father. One day after school, she and another friend were watching television with Michael. Craig came in and became furious with Michael because he had left some laundry unfolded on the sofa. To avoid further embarrassment for Michael, she and the friend left the room. Several minutes later, Craig called them back in. He said, "I'm done thumping on him now." Michael had red marks all over his face and neck. This was not the last time Jennifer saw marks on Michael's body. She tried to get Michael out of the house as much as possible. She recalled one evening when she called Craig asking permission for Michael to go for a walk. Each time she called, Craig remarked that Michael could go if she would bring along a dog leash. Jennifer ignored the comment thinking it was just another way for Craig to belittle his son. However, on this particular evening, Craig sounded different. Knowing he was serious, she found a yellow rope in the garage and took it along with her. She believed this was just another silly little game they would have to play to get Michael out of the house. When Jennifer arrived at the Alborgeden's, Michael and his father were in the living room. Craig told Jennifer to tie the rope like a lasso and she agreed. He put the rope around Michael's neck and made him leave the house on all fours, like a dog. Jennifer was horrified but held the other end of the rope.

Michael's friends came to a point where they could no longer tolerate Craig's abusive behavior toward Michael. After much persuasion, they convinced Michael to discuss the situation with the school vice-principal, Mr. Hastings. They accompanied him into the office for the meeting. As soon as they had taken their seats, Mr. Hastings asked Michael if he was being abused by anyone. When Michael didn't respond, he turned to Jennifer and asked her if she thought Michael was being abused. She replied, "Yes, Michael is being abused." Hastings turned to Michael and said to him, "I don't like you, and if you're not going to say anything, you can just leave." Michael finally broke down and told the truth. Michael and his friends detected the vice-principal's skepticism and Hastings ended the meeting by saying, "I hope you don't think you could just bullshit me around for nothing." This was not the meeting that Michael and his friends anticipated because Mr. Hastings had reacted as if Michael had done something wrong to warrant the abuse.

Michael now knew that escaping his father's abuse was almost virtually impossible. He had nowhere to turn, and not including his friends, no one believed he was being abused.

Several weeks later, Mr. Hastings requested a meeting with Michael and his father. Michael prayed that finally he would get help, that someone would take action against his father. Once again the meeting was not what Michael expected or hoped it to be. Hastings sat on the opposite side of the room with Michael's probation officer, Ms. Haller, from an earlier charge of break and entering. Michael sat beside his father.   Hastings asked Michael, "are you being abused in the home?" Michael looked at his father and lowered his head. He quietly replied, "no."

Michael wrote a poem to his father a year before he killed him.

FATHER AND A SON

A father and me is closer than

the wind blowing against a tree

closer than the fish and the sea.

For with no father there would be no me.

And I hope my Father can see that my love

is stronger than if we were

three. Father I am telling you

this because I want you to love me.

So just remember Father these words

are coming from me, "I love you so

much I just hope you can see."

love always,

Michael

After Craig read the poem, he tearfully confided to a friend that he didn't know how to love his son. He wished he could show affection instead of hitting him. He concluded, "But that's the way my dad brought me up. Never in my whole life did my father ever tell me, "I love you."

Once the divorce papers were finalized, Michael became depressed and angry at his mother for leaving him with his father. He hated her. He hated his father and he hated his life in general. On that fateful Friday evening, Michael didn't get home until one-thirty in the morning. He had gone skating with some friends and was supposed to be home shortly after eleven. He was late, and he knew that his father would be very angry. When Michael came in, his father was lying on the couch, apparently asleep. As Michael quietly walked past to go to his bedroom, his father yelled, "you always gotta push it. Every time I give you a break, you always gotta push it! Come out here!"

Craig then told Michael he had two choices,

"you kill me, or I kill you." As Michael continued to walk to his room, he heard the cocking of a rifle. When he turned back, he found himself looking down the barrel of a gun. Craig threatened Michael again and although he didn't believe his dad was serious, he took the weapon from him. Craig began taunting him. "I hate you. You're not my son! I never intended to have you. I hate your mother. If you don't kill me, I'm going to kill you, then kill her, and then kill myself!" Without even thinking, Michael shot his father. He couldn't remember how many times he pulled the trigger. He recalled later, "After I pulled the first time I kind of like blanked out ... I just kept pulling it until it stopped firing anymore."

In April, 1985, Michael Alborgeden filed a missing person's report on his father, Craig Alborgeden and told the authorities that he hadn't heard from or seen his father in four days. A few days after the report had been filed, a fisherman found Craig Alborgeden's body under a marina dock. The body had been shot multiple times. It was determined that Craig died about four to five days earlier. Within hours, Michael Alborgeden was arrested for the murder of his father.   Michael received the maximum prison time allowable, four years for involuntary manslaughter. He would also serve another two years for using a gun in the commission of the crime. Due to the fact that he was only sixteen at the time, he would serve his sentence in a facility for youthful offenders.

Chapter 5: School Shootings Intro

The U.S. Department of Education reported that, in 1997, nearly 6,300 students were expelled from American schools for carrying firearms. As evidenced by many of the recent reports about school violence, several students chose to express their anger in caustic ways.

Many schools have responded to the threat of increasing violence by tightening security, installing spiked fences, motorized gates, bulletproof metal-covered doors, metal detectors, and security guards who search student desks and lockers. Some students and even faculty complain that this only creates prisons out of the schools. Most schools have hired more counselors and violence prevention coordinators.

Besides prescription drugs, few preventative

efforts are being made to help students with the various psychological and emotional needs they may have before they erupt into a crisis situation. Sometimes teenagers see no alternative but violence to solve their escalating internal and, sometimes, external problems.

Revenge seems to be a common thread that runs through all of these massacres. Retribution is rooted in a sense of real or perceived injustice towards the perpetrator of the shooting. Many school shootings are generated by a desire for revenge against society, fed by a simmering anger over being denied a perceived entitlement to respect or personal recognition.

All of the teenage school shooters have been deeply influenced by mass media, usually in the form of video games and movies. Both media forms tend to be very vivid, intense, and increasingly violent. Teenagers growing up in the late 20th century and early 21st are immersed in an extremely hostile environment for the mind. This mental environment is especially hazardous for the young mind that is not fully developed, lacking the experience needed for balance and proportional decision-making.

When kids suffer abuse at home from parents and siblings, they often then go to school and suffer bullying from peers and an endless series of dictates from teachers. They begin to feel trapped as they can't avoid abuse no matter where they turn. In addition, they see that the authority at home is part of the problem, and authority at school is either unconcerned or inadequate at helping them. They gradually realize that authority is fundamentally two-faced as it is not based on kind guidance as officially stated, but instead is based on controlling and exploiting the less powerful.

Consequently, these kids begin to perceive that the world is towering over them and abusing the weak. Feeling trapped and powerless, they naturally search for a way out. The easiest and most effective way to acquire power is to obtain something powerful like a gun. Kids easily believe that using a gun is an effective method for resolving their problems. Every movie, video game, and television show they watch depicts the world through this foolish one-dimensional lens of power expression and problem resolution via deadly violence. These kids believe that it is acceptable to mimic these performances at a school shooting as other students have set this precedent.

Chapter 6: Virginia Tech Massacre

Seung-Hui Cho

Born on January 18th, 1984, at the time of his rampage, Cho was a senior-level undergraduate student at Virginia Polytechnic Institute and State.

In middle school, he was diagnosed with a severe anxiety disorder known as Selective Mutism, as well as a major depressive disorder. After his diagnosis, he began receiving treatment, and continued to receive therapy and special education support until his junior year of high school. Two students complained to authorities about the behavior of Cho in separate incidents in 2005. Police questioned Cho and he was sent to a mental health facility, but no charges were filed against him.

General District Court records show that a Montgomery County magistrate ordered Cho, then twenty-three years old, to undergo a mental evaluation in December of 2005. The magistrate found probable cause that Cho was "mentally ill," and an "imminent danger to him and others," seriously mentally ill enough as to be unable to care for himself.

The police spoke with acquaintances of Cho and became concerned that he might be suicidal. Officers suggested to Cho that he speak to a counselor, and Cho took their advice. Based on his meeting with the counselor, Cho went to the police department voluntarily; a temporary detention order was obtained, and Cho was taken to a mental health facility, the Carilion Saint Albans Behavioral Health Center.

During Cho's last two years at Virginia Tech, several instances of his abnormal behavior, including plays and other writings he submitted, contained references to violence that caused concern among teachers and classmates. Detectives believe that Cho Seung-Hui was obsessed with eighteen year old student Emily Hilscher, one of his first two victims. Cho apparently had become infatuated by her.

Dressed more like a boy scout than a mass murderer, Cho arrived at Hilscher's dormitory room early Monday morning on April 16th. It is unclear whether Emily Hilscher had responded to her killer's approaches. Cho, jealous of Emily's boyfriend, gunned her down. Another student,

Ryan Clark, rushed to help after hearing his neighbor arguing with Cho, and the twenty-two year old died alongside her.

Cho then went back to his room where he used his computer to assemble an 1800 word written statement, videos, and photographs of himself, which he then packaged up and mailed for overnight delivery to NBC news in New York via the small post office near the main gates of the campus. The package was time stamped at 9:01 a.m. He then went back to his dorm room and collected his weapons.

Around 9:45 a.m., two hours after his first killings, Cho entered Norris Hall and proceeded to chain the three main exits to the building shut. He placed a note on at least one of the chained doors, claiming that any attempts to open the door would cause a bomb to explode. In Room 206, professor G.V. Loganathan was teaching advanced hydrology when he was shot and killed by Cho along with nine students; another two were injured.

In Room 207, professor Christopher James Bishop was teaching Elementary German when Cho burst into the room, shot the professor, and killed four students in the first row of the classroom, wounding another six.

In the stairwell, Cho fired at Janitor Gene Cole and missed five times, according to the janitor. Cho then moved on to Norris 204 where Cho was initially prevented from entering by barricades erected by instructors and students. Professor Liviu Librescu, a Holocaust survivor, forcibly prevented Cho from entering the room. Librescu was able to hold the door closed until most of his students escaped through the windows, but he died after being shot multiple times through the door. Student, Nicole Regina

White, was also killed while another student was injured.

Cho proceeded to Room 211 where Professor Jocelyne Couture-Nowak was teaching Intermediate French. Again, people attempted to block the door, but the Professor and another student were killed.

Students, including Zach Petkewicz, barricaded the door of room 205 with a large table after substitute professor Haiyan Cheng and a student saw Cho heading toward them. Cho shot several times through the door but failed to force his way in. No one in that classroom was wounded or killed.

Hearing the commotion on the floor below, Professor Kevin Granata brought twenty students from a nearby classroom into a third-floor office where the door could be locked. He then went downstairs to investigate and Cho fatally shot him. None of the students locked in Granata's office were injured.

Virginia Tech and Blacksburg police spent three minutes dashing across campus to the scene. They then began the process of assembling a team, clearing the area, and trying to break through the doors, which took another five minutes. After they blasted through the chained doors with shotguns, Cho put a bullet through his head and died in a classroom alongside thirty of his victims.

In total, Cho fired 174 rounds of ammunition. Each student killed was shot at least three times each.

The police enter the scene to find Cho dead and in possession of a 9mm semi-automatic and a .22 caliber handgun, as well as multiple rounds of ammunition and several knives. Among the items found in Cho's backpack was prescription medication for treatment of psychological problems and a note denouncing "rich kids."

Chapter 7: Texas Tower Sniper

Charles Whitman

Charles Joseph Whitman, born June 24th, 1941, was a student at the University of Texas and a former Marine. He grew up in an upper-middle class family headed by a father who owned a successful plumbing business in Lake Worth, Florida. Whitman excelled academically and was well liked by his peers and neighbors. There were underlying dysfunctional issues within his family, however, that escalated in

1966 when his mother left his father and moved to Texas. The older Whitman was a controlling man who was known to become physically and emotionally abusive to his wife and children.

Charles Whitman's frustrations with his dysfunctional family were complicated by abuse of amphetamines and health issues including headaches. A glioblastoma, a highly aggressive brain tumor, was discovered during Whitman's autopsy. Experts have concluded that it may have played a role in his actions. Whitman was also affected by a court martial as a United States Marine, his failings as a student at the University of Texas, his ambitious personal expectations, and his psychotic mental state.

Several months prior to the shootings, he was summoned to Lake Worth, Florida, to pick up his mother who was filing for divorce from his father. The stress caused by the break-up of the family became the dominant discussion between Whitman and a psychiatrist at the University of Texas Health Center on March 29th, 1966.

Whitman enrolled in the mechanical engineering program at the University of Texas on September 15th, 1961, through a USMC scholarship. His hobbies at this point included karate, scuba diving, and hunting. This last hobby got him into trouble at the University when he shot a deer, dragged it to his dormitory, and skinned it in his shower. Due to this incident, and sub-standard grades, Whitman's scholarship was withdrawn in 1963.

In August 1962, Whitman married Kathleen Frances Leissner, another University of Texas student, in a wedding that was held in Leissner's hometown of Needville, Texas. The following year, he returned to active duty at Marine Corps Base Camp Lejeune, North Carolina, where he was both promoted to Lance Corporal and involved in an accident in which his Jeep rolled over an embankment.

In November of 1962, Whitman was court-martialed for gambling, possessing a personal firearm on base, and threatening another Marine over a thirty dollar loan for which Whitman demanded fifteen dollars interest. He was sentenced to thirty days of confinement, ninety days of hard labor, and demoted to the rank of Private.

In December, 1964, honorably discharged from the Marines, Whitman returned to the University of Texas and enrolled in the Architectural Engineering program. He worked as a bill collector for Standard Finance and later as a bank teller at Austin National Bank. In January, 1965, he took a temporary job with Central Freight Lines and worked as a traffic surveyor for the Texas Highway Department. He also volunteered as a Scoutmaster for Austin Scout Troop five while Kathy worked as a biology teacher at Lanier High School.

In May of 1966, Whitman's mother contacted Charles and because of several disagreements she had with his father, she announced she was filing for a divorce. Whitman drove to Florida to help his mother move to back to Austin, where she found work in a cafeteria. The move prompted his youngest brother, John, to leave Lake Worth as well, but his brother Patrick decided to continue living at home and working for their father at his plumbing supply business.

Whitman's father began to telephone him several times a week, pleading with him to convince his mother to return to Lake Worth, but Charles refused. The day before the shootings, Whitman purchased binoculars and a knife from a hardware store, and Spam from a 7-Eleven. He then picked up his wife from her summer job as a Bell operator, and met his mother for lunch at the Wyatt Cafeteria near the campus.

Around 4:00 p.m., on July 31st, they visited friends, John and Fran Morgan, who lived in the same neighborhood, leaving at approximately 5:50 so that Kathy Whitman wouldn't be late for her 6:00–10:00 p.m. shift that night. At 6:45, Whitman began typing his suicide note, a portion of which read:

I do not quite understand what it is that compels me to type this letter. Perhaps it is to leave some vague reason for the actions I have recently performed. I do not really understand myself these days. I am supposed to be an average reasonable and intelligent young man. However, lately (I cannot recall when it started) I have been a victim of many unusual and irrational thoughts.

The note explained that he had decided to murder both his mother and his wife, but made no mention of the coming attacks at the university. Expressing uncertainty about his actual reasons, he nevertheless observed that he felt he wanted to relieve Kathy and his mother Margaret from the suffering of the world.

Just after midnight, Whitman rendered his mother unconscious and then stabbed her in the heart. He left a handwritten note beside her body, which read in part:

To Whom It May Concern: I have just taken my mother's life. I am very upset over having done it. However, I feel that if there is a heaven she is definitely there now...I am truly sorry...Let there be no doubt in your mind that I loved this woman with all my heart.

Whitman returned to his home at 906 Jewell

Street and stabbed his wife Kathy three times in the heart as she slept, returning to the typewritten note he had begun earlier, which he then finished by hand, writing,

I imagine it appears that I brutally killed both of my loved ones. I was only trying to do a quick thorough job...If my life insurance policy is valid please pay off my debts, donate the rest anonymously to a mental health foundation. Maybe research can prevent further tragedies of this type.

Whitman also requested that an autopsy be done after his death to determine if there had been anything to explain his actions and increasing headaches. He also wrote notes to each of his brothers and his father, and left instructions in the apartment that the two canisters of film he left on the table should be developed, and that the puppy, Schocie, should be given to Kathy's parents.

At 5:45 a.m. on Monday, August 1st, 1966, Whitman phoned Kathy's supervisor at Bell to explain that she was sick and could not make her shift that day. He made a similar phone call to Margaret's workplace about five hours later.

Whitman rented a hand truck from Austin Rental Company and cashed $250 of worthless checks at the bank before going to Davis' Hardware and purchasing an M1 carbine, explaining that he wanted to go hunting for wild hogs. He then went to Sears and purchased a shotgun and a green rifle case. After sawing off the shotgun barrel – while chatting with the mail carrier – Whitman packed it with a Remington 700 6mm bolt-action hunting rifle with a 4x Leupold Scope, an M1 carbine, a Remington .35 caliber pump rifle, and various other equipment, in a wooden crate and his Marine footlocker. He also had a .357 Magnum revolver, 9mm German Luger, and another small caliber pistol on his person.

Before heading to the tower, Whitman donned khaki coveralls over his shirt and jeans. Pushing the rented dolly carrying his equipment, he met security guard Jack Rodman and obtained a parking pass, claiming he had a delivery to make. He showed Rodman a card identifying him as a research assistant for the school.

Whitman entered the Main Building shortly after 11:30 a.m. He struggled with the elevator until an employee, Vera Palmer, informed him that it had not been powered and turned it on for him. He thanked her and took the elevator to the 27th floor of the tower, just one floor beneath the clock face.

Whitman then lugged the dolly up one long

flight of stairs to the hallway that led to a doglegged stairway that went up to the observation deck area. Edna Townsley, the receptionist on duty, observing Whitman's trunk, asked if he had his University work identification. Whitman knocked her unconscious with the butt of his rifle and dragged her body behind a sofa. She later died from her injuries at Seton Hospital. Moments later, Cheryl Botts and Don Walden, a young couple who had been sightseeing on the deck, returned to the receptionist area and encountered Whitman holding a rifle in each hand. Botts later claimed that she believed that the large red stain on the floor was varnish, and that Whitman was there to shoot pigeons. Whitman and the young couple exchanged hellos and the couple left for the elevators. When they were gone, Whitman barricaded the stairway and donned his white sweatband.

Two families, the Gabours and Lamports, were on their way up the stairs when they encountered Whitman's barricade. Michael Gabour was attempting to look beyond the barricade when Whitman fired the sawed-off shotgun at him, hitting him in the left side of his neck and shoulder region, sending him over the staircase railing onto other family members. Whitman fired the sawed-off shotgun two more times through grates on the stairway into the families as they tried to run back down the stairs. Mark Gabour and his aunt, Marguerite Lamport, died instantly. Michael was partially disabled and his mother was permanently disabled.

The first shots from the tower's outer deck came at approximately 11:48 a.m. A history professor was the first to phone the Austin Police Department after he saw several students in the South Mall center gunned down. Many others had dismissed the rifle reports, not realizing there was directed gunfire. Eventually, the shootings caused panic as news spread and all active police officers in Austin were ordered to the campus. Other off-duty officers, Travis County Sheriff's deputies, and Texas Department of Public Safety troopers, also converged on the area to assist.

About twenty minutes later, once Whitman began facing return fire from the authorities and armed civilians who had brought out their personal firearms to assist police, he used the waterspouts on each side of the tower as gun ports. These allowed him to continue shooting largely protected from the gunfire below, but it greatly limited his range of targets below.

Ramiro Martinez, an officer who participated that morning, later stated that the civilian shooters should be credited as they made it difficult for Whitman to take careful aim. Police lieutenant Marion Lee, reporting from a small airplane, noted that there was a single sniper firing from the observation deck. The airplane circled the tower while Lee tried to shoot Whitman, but turbulence made it difficult for him to get a clear shot. The airplane, piloted by Jim Boutwell, was hit by Whitman's rifle fire but continued to circle the tower from a safe distance until the end of the incident.

Whitman's choice of victims was indiscriminate. Most were shot on Guadalupe Street, a major commercial and business district across from the west side of the campus. Efforts to reach and rescue the wounded included an armored car and ambulances run by local funeral homes. Ambulance driver Morris Hohmann was responding to victims on West 23rd Street when he was shot in the leg. The bullet severed an artery, and another ambulance driver quickly attended to Hohmann, taking him about ten blocks south of UT to Brackenridge Hospital, the only local emergency room.

The Brackenridge Administrator declared an emergency and medical staff raced to reinforce the on-duty shifts. Following the shootings, volunteers donated blood at both Brackenridge and the Travis County Blood Bank. Austin Police Department (APD) Officers Ramiro Martinez, Houston McCoy, Jerry Day, and civilian Allen Crum, were the first to reach the tower's observation deck, stepping outside the south door at 1:24 p.m. Martinez, closely followed by McCoy, formed one team and proceeded north on the east deck. Day, followed by Crum, formed a second team and proceeded west on the south deck, with Whitman believed to be between the two teams.

Several feet before reaching the southwest

corner, Crum accidentally discharged a shot from his borrowed rifle. At the same time, Martinez jumped around the corner into the northeast area and rapidly fired all six rounds from his .38 police revolver at Whitman. As Martinez was firing, McCoy jumped out to the right and fired two fatal shots of double buckshot with his 12-gauge shotgun into the head, neck, and left side of Whitman, who had been sitting with his back toward the north wall in the northwest corner area, fifty feet away.

Whitman, who appeared to be unaware of the presence of Martinez and McCoy, was partially shielded by the deck tower lights, and in a position to defend assaults from either corner.

After firing six rounds, Martinez threw his empty revolver onto the deck and grabbed McCoy's shotgun. He ran to Whitman's prone body and fired directly Whitman's upper left arm.

Martinez then threw the shotgun on the deck and hurriedly left the scene, repeatedly shouting, "I got him."

After attending to the wounded in the stairwell, APD Officers Milton Shoquist, Harold Moe, and George Shepard, made their way up the stairs to join APD Officer, Phillip Conner, and Texas Department of Public Safety Agent, W.A. Cowan. Arriving on the 28th floor as Martinez, McCoy, Day, and Crum were outside on the observation deck, Moe, with a hand-held radio, heard Martinez as he ran past shouting "I got him," and relayed his words to the APD radio dispatcher. Houston McCoy appeared before the Travis County Grand Jury on August 5th, 1966, and received a justifiable killing verdict for the death of Whitman. At the Cook Funeral Home the next day, an autopsy was performed and an Astrocytoma brain tumor was discovered in Whitman. Due to his status as a veteran Marine,

Whitman had a casket draped with an American flag for his burial.

Chapter 8: Columbine High School

Dylan Klebold and Eric Harris

Dylan Klebold was born September 11th, 1981, in Lakewood, Colorado, to Thomas and Susan Klebold. Thomas Klebold was a geophysicist turned realtor and ran a small real estate business from home. Susan Klebold worked for the State of Colorado, administering training programs for the disabled.

Eric Harris was born April 9th, 1981 in Wichita, Kansas, to Wayne and Katherine Harris. His father was a US Air Force Transport Pilot and his mother a homemaker. They moved to Columbine, Colorado, in 1996 where Eric met Dylan in Junior High.

In 1996, Eric Harris created a private website on America Online. The site was originally set up to host Doom levels that he and Dylan Klebold had created, mainly for friends. The blog postings, however, began to show the first signs of Harris' ever-growing anger against society. Harris's site had few visitors, and caused no concern until late 1997, when Dylan Klebold gave the address to Brooks Brown, Harris's former friend. Brown's mother had filed numerous complaints with the Jefferson County Sheriff's office about Eric Harris, believing him to be dangerous.

The website was filled with death threats towards Brooks, and Dylan knew that if Brooks had the address, it would eventually be seen by his mother, and possibly result in problems for Harris. Indeed, Brooks Brown's parents contacted the Jefferson County Sheriff's Office, and investigator Michael Guerra was notified of the site. Guerra discovered the website contained violent threats directed at the students and teachers of Columbine High School. Other material included blurbs Harris had written concerning his hatred of society in general, and his desire to kill those who annoyed him. Harris began noting the completion of pipe bombs on his site, and included a gun count and hit-list of individuals he wished to target. He never, however, detailed his overall plan. As Harris had admitted to having explosives, Guerra wrote a draft affidavit for a search warrant of the Harris household, but it was never filed.

In early 1998, Eric Harris and Dylan Klebold were caught with tools and equipment they'd stolen moments earlier from a parked van near Littleton, Colorado. Both were arrested and attended a joint court hearing where they pleaded guilty to the felony theft. The judge sentenced them to juvenile diversion where they attended various classes together, including a class on anger management. Harris started attending therapy with a psychologist, and continued to do so for about a year. Harris and Klebold were eventually released from diversion several weeks early due to their good behavior, although they remained on probation.

At a meeting with his psychiatrist, Harris complained of depression, anger, and suicidal thoughts, and was prescribed the anti-depressant Zoloft. He complained about restlessness and a lack of concentration to his doctor, and in April was switched to a similar drug, Luvox. At the time of his death, Harris had therapeutic Luvox levels in his system. Some analysts have argued that one or both of these medications may have contributed to Harris's actions as these drugs have a noted side-effect of causing increased aggression, loss of remorse, depersonalization, and mania, in some people.

In the months prior to the attacks, Harris and Klebold acquired two 9mm semi-automatic handguns and two 12-gauge shotguns. A rifle and the two shotguns were bought by a friend, Robyn Anderson, at the Tanner Gun Show in December, 1998. Harris and Klebold later bought a handgun from another friend, Mark Manes, for $500. Manes was jailed after the massacre for selling a handgun to a minor, as was Philip Duran, who had introduced the duo to Manes.

With instructions from the Internet, Harris and Klebold built ninety-nine improvised explosive devices (IEDs) of various designs and size, and sawed the barrels and butts from their shotguns to make them easier to conceal. Numerous felony violations of state and federal law, including the National Firearms Act and the Gun Control Act of 1968, were conducted even before the massacre began.

Harris and Klebold both began keeping journals of their progress soon after their arrests, and documented their arsenal with video. Journal entries revealed that the pair had an elaborate plan for a major bombing rivaling that of the Oklahoma City bombing, plans drawn up for ways to escape to Mexico, a plot that involved hijacking an aircraft at Denver International Airport to crash it into a building in New York City, as well as details for the school attacks. The pair envisioned that after setting off bombs in the cafeteria at the busiest time of day, killing many hundreds of students, they

Whoa before 9/11

would use their guns to shoot survivors as they fled from the school. Then, as police cars, ambulances, fire trucks, and reporters came to the school, bombs in the boys' cars would explode, killing emergency personnel, media, and law officers. This original plan failed when their main explosives did not detonate.

The boys kept videos that documented the explosives, ammunition, and weapons they had acquired illegally. In these videos, the shooters revealed all the elaborate and creative ways they had thought up to hide their arsenals in their own homes, as well as how they misled their parents. Some videos contained footage of the pair doing target practice in nearby foothills, and shots of the high school they planned to attack. On April 20th, approximately thirty minutes before the attack, they shot a final video saying goodbye, and apologizing to their friends and families.

During the shootings, Harris fired the following weapons:

- 12 gauge Savage-Springfield 67H pump-action shotgun; twenty-five rounds fired.

- Hi-Point 995 Carbine 9mm semi-automatic rifle; fired 96 times.

Harris committed suicide by shooting himself in the head with his shotgun.

Klebold fired the following weapons:

- 9mm Intratec TEC-9 semi-automatic handgun; fifty-five rounds fired.

- 12-gauge Stevens 311D double-barreled sawed-off.

Klebold committed suicide with a shot to the left temple with the TEC-9.

At 11:10 a.m. on Tuesday, April 20th, 1999, Eric Harris and Dylan Klebold arrived at

Columbine High School in separate cars. Harris parked in the junior student parking lot, Klebold in the senior student parking lot, neither at spaces assigned to them. From these spots, both of them had excellent views of the cafeteria's side entrance, and each shooter was covering a main exit of the school. Shortly before arriving, Harris and Klebold set up a small firebomb in a field about half a mile away from the school. The bomb was set to explode at 11:14 a.m., and is thought to have been placed there as a diversion for emergency personnel. The bomb did partially detonate, causing a small fire that was extinguished by the fire department.

The pair met near Harris' car. Armed with two twenty-pound propane bombs in duffel bags, the pair entered the cafeteria a few minutes before lunch and placed the bags carrying the bombs inside. Each bomb was set to explode at approximately 11:17 a.m. Coincidentally, a custodian removed the security camera video tape, rewound it, and placed a new tape in the slot around the same time they entered the cafeteria.

The shooters returned to their cars to wait until the bombs exploded, intending to open fire on students fleeing the school through the main entrances after the cafeteria bombs detonated. As they returned to their cars, Harris encountered Brooks Brown, a classmate with whom he had recently patched up longstanding disagreements. Brown was surprised to see Harris as Harris had been absent from class that morning. Brown told Harris that he had missed a test, but Harris seemed unconcerned. Harris then warned him, "Brooks, I like you now. Get out of here. Go home." Brown, feeling uneasy, walked away. Several minutes later, students departing Columbine for lunch noticed Brooks Brown heading down South Pierce Street, away from the school.

Meanwhile, Harris and Klebold armed themselves by their cars and waited for the bombs to explode. When the cafeteria bombs failed, Harris and Klebold armed themselves with their weapons, met, and walked toward the building. They went to the top of the West Entrance steps, the highest point on campus. From this vantage point, the cafeteria's side entrance was at the bottom of the staircase, the school's main West Entrance was to their left, and the athletic fields were to their right.

At 11:19 a.m., a witness heard Eric Harris yell, "Go! Go!" At that moment, the gunmen pulled their guns and Harris began shooting at Rachel Scott and Richard Castaldo with his 9mm semi-automatic carbine rifle, who were sitting on a grassy knoll to their left, eating lunch. Scott was hit four times and killed instantly. Castaldo, hit eight times, was critically wounded. It is unclear who shot first and who killed Scott. Subsequently, many rumors have swirled regarding the causes of the rampage, suggesting the possible targeting of Christians. One such rumor included the shooters asking Scott if she believed in God, and then killing her after she answered that she did. The FBI later concluded that this conversation did not take place.

Harris removed his trench coat and took out his 9mm rifle again, aiming it down the West Staircase. Daniel Rohrbough and two friends, Sean Graves and Lance Kirklin, were walking up the staircase directly below the shooters. Kirklin reported seeing them at the top when suddenly they began shooting at him. All three fell, wounded.

Harris and Klebold then turned and began shooting south, away from the school, at students sitting on the grassy knoll adjacent to the steps, opposite the West Entrance of the school. Michael Johnson was hit, but kept running and escaped. Mark Taylor fell to the ground, crippled, and played dead. The other three escaped uninjured. As the shooting continued, Sean Graves stood up and limped down the staircase to the cafeteria's side entrance, where he collapsed in front of the door. Klebold walked down the steps, heading toward the cafeteria. As he descended, he shot Lance Kirklin once more in the face, critically wounding him. As Daniel Rohrbough struggled down the steps towards the bottom of the staircase, Klebold walked up to him and shot him in the back at close range, killing him. He then continued down the staircase and entered the cafeteria, walking over the injured Sean Graves, who lay at the cafeteria entrance. It is speculated that Klebold did this because he was checking to see why the propane bombs had failed to explode. As Klebold stepped into the cafeteria, Harris began to shoot down the steps at several students who'd been sitting near the cafeteria's entrance, wounding Anne-Marie Hochhalter as she attempted to flee. After a few seconds, Klebold returned up the staircase to meet with Harris at the top.

The two then shot toward students standing near the soccer field a few yards away, but did not hit anyone. They threw pipe bombs as they made their way towards the West Entrance, none of which detonated. Inside the campus, teacher Patti Nielson, seeing the commotion, walked towards the West Entrance with student Brian Anderson. She wanted to walk outside and tell the two students to "Knock it off," as she thought they were shooting a video or pulling a prank. As Anderson opened the first set of double doors, Harris and Klebold shot out the windows. Anderson was injured by flying glass and Nielson was hit in the shoulder by shrapnel. Reacting in fear, she quickly stood up and ran down the hall into the library, where she alerted the students inside, demanding they duck beneath desks and remain silent. She then dialed 911 and concealed herself beneath the library's administrative counter. Brian Anderson remained behind, caught between the exterior and interior doors.

Soon thereafter, at approximately 11:24 a.m., a Jefferson County deputy sheriff arrived at the scene and began shooting at Harris and Klebold, distracting them from the injured Brian Anderson. Anderson staggered out of the area and made it into the library where he ran into an open staff break room. He remained there until the ordeal ended. Harris fired ten shots at the officer, who then radioed in a Code 33 (officer in need of emergency assistance). When his gun ran out of ammunition, Harris ran inside the school with Klebold. The pair then proceeded down the main North Hallway, shooting at anyone they saw and throwing pipe bombs. While doing so, they shot student Stephanie Munson in the ankle. She was able to walk out of the school and made it to a house across the street.

Moments earlier, Coach Dave Sanders had evacuated the cafeteria through a staircase leading up to the second floor. The staircase was around the corner from the Library Hallway in the main South Hallway. He and a student turned the corner and were walking down the Library Hallway when they saw the shooters coming around the corner from the North Hallway. The two quickly turned around and ran the other way. The shooters came around the corner and Harris shot at both of them, hitting Dave Sanders in the chest as he reached the

South Hallway, but he missed the student. The student ran into a science classroom and alerted the teacher inside.

Meanwhile, the shooters returned up the North Hallway. Coach Sanders struggled over to the science classroom where thirty students had been taking an exam, and the teacher took him in. A sign was placed in the exterior window that read, "I am bleeding to death," in order to alert police of their location. Two students administered first aid, and attempted to control the bleeding with the shirts of the male students in the room. A teacher and several students remained in contact with police outside of the school using a phone in the classroom. All the students in the science room were evacuated safely, but Sanders was not evacuated, and died at approximately 3:00 p.m. He was the only teacher killed in the ordeal.

As the shooting unfolded, Patti Nielson was on the phone with emergency services, recounting her experience, and trying to get students to take cover under desks. According to transcripts, her call was received by the 911 operator at 11:25 a.m. The time between the call being answered and the shooters entering the library was four minutes and ten seconds. Before entering, the shooters threw two bombs into the cafeteria from the staircase in the South Hallway, both of which exploded. One can be seen on the security tapes. They then threw another into the Library Hallway, which also exploded, luckily only damaging some lockers.

At 11:29 a.m., Harris and Klebold entered the library where fifty-two students, two teachers, and two librarians were hiding. As he entered, Harris shot at a display case at the opposite end of the administrative counter, injuring student Evan Todd, who was hiding under a copier table nearby. Harris then yelled for everyone to "Get up!" so loudly that he can be heard on the 911 recording at 11:29:18. Staff and students hiding in the library exterior rooms said they heard the gunmen say things like "Everyone with white hats, stand up! This is for all the shit you've given us for the past four years!" and "All jocks stand up! We'll get the guys in white hats!" Wearing a white baseball cap at Columbine was a tradition amongst sports team members.

When no one stood up, Harris was heard saying, "Fine, I'll start shooting anyway!" He fired his shotgun at a desk, not knowing Evan Todd was under it. Todd was hit by wood splinters, but not seriously hurt. The shooters made their way to the opposite side of the library, to the two rows of computers. Evan Todd used the time to conceal himself behind the administrative counter. Kyle Velasquez was sitting at the north end of the computers. Police said that he had not hidden under the desk, but that he was curled up under the computer table. Klebold shot at him first, hitting him in the head and back, killing him. The shooters set down their duffel bags filled with ammunition at the row of computers, and reloaded their weapons.

They then walked to the windows facing the outside staircase, where they'd come from just minutes ago. Noticing police evacuating students, Harris said, "Let's go kill some cops," and they began to shoot out the windows. Police returned fire. After a few seconds, Klebold turned away from the windows and fired his shotgun at a nearby table, injuring Patrick Ireland, Daniel Steepleton, and Makai Hall. He immediately removed his trench coat. Harris grabbed his shotgun and walked over to the lower row of computer desks, firing his gun underneath the first desk in the row without looking to see who was under it. The shot killed

Steven Curnow, who was hiding underneath. He then shot under the next computer desk, injuring Kacey Ruegsegger.

Harris walked over to the table across from the lower computer row, slapped the top twice with his hand, knelt down, and said "peek-a-boo," before shooting Cassie Bernall in the head. The recoil from the weapon hit his face, breaking his nose. Although one witness reported that Bernall was the individual who was asked, "Do you believe in God?" the exchange actually happened with Klebold and surviving student Valeen Schnurr. Three students witnessed Bernall's death, including the person who was hiding under the table with her, and testified that Klebold and Bernall did not exchange words. Although some students who were in the library asserted the exchange occurred, none of them physically witnessed it. They may instead have heard the exchange between Klebold and

Schnurr and have been misled by news reports that attributed the words to Bernall.

Harris turned to the next table where student Bree Pasquale sat next to the table rather than beneath it. She had not hidden underneath, as there was not enough room. Harris asked her if she wanted to die, and Pasquale responded with a plea for her life. Witnesses report that Harris seemed disoriented, possibly from the wound to his face, which was bleeding heavily. As Harris taunted Pasquale, Patrick Ireland tried to aid Makai Hall, who had suffered a wound to his knee. While doing so, his head came above the table. Klebold shot him, hitting him twice in the head and once in the foot. He was knocked unconscious, but survived.

Klebold then proceeded towards another set of tables, discovering Isaiah Shoels, Matthew Kechter, and Craig Scott, Rachel Scott's brother, hiding under the table. All were popular athletes at the school. Klebold attempted to pull Isaiah out from underneath the table, but was unsuccessful. He then called to Harris, who left Bree Pasquale and joined him. Klebold and Harris taunted Shoels for a few seconds and made derogatory racial comments towards him before Harris knelt down and shot him in the chest at close range, killing him. Klebold also knelt down and opened fire, hitting and killing Matthew Kechter. Craig Scott remained uninjured but he lay in the blood of his friends, pretending to be dead.

Harris turned and threw a CO2 bomb at the table where Hall, Steepleton, and Ireland were located. The CO2 bomb landed on Daniel Steepleton's thigh, but Makai Hall grabbed the bomb and threw it south, away from the shooters.

Harris walked to the bookcases between the west and center section of tables in the library. He jumped on one of the bookcases and shook it, then shot at something in that general area. It is not known what he shot at, since no one could see him at the time. Klebold walked through the main area, past the first set of bookcases, the central desk area, and a second set of bookcases, into the east area. Harris met up with him there. Klebold shot out a display case next to the door, turned, and shot at the closest table to him, injuring Mark Kintgen. He turned to the table to his left and shot at it, injuring Lisa Kreutz and Val Schnurr with the same bullet. He approached the table and fired again, killing Lauren Townsend. Meanwhile, Harris went over to another table where two girls were hiding, bent down to look at them, and dismissed them as 'pathetic.' The shooters then went over to an empty table and reloaded their weapons. Schnurr, who had been hurt badly, began to cry out at that point, "Oh, God help me!" Klebold went back to her and asked her if she believed in God. She floundered in her answer, saying no and then yes, trying to get the answer right. He asked her why and she said it was because it was what her family believed. He taunted her, reloaded his shotgun, and then walked away. The slightly injured Evan Todd reported that Klebold said, "God is gay."

Harris moved to another table and shot twice underneath it, injuring Nicole Nowlen and John Tomlin. When Tomlin tried to crawl out, Klebold came back around the corner and kicked him.

Harris taunted his attempt at escape, and Klebold shot him repeatedly, killing him. Harris walked back over to the other side of the table where Lauren Townsend lay. Behind it, Kelly Fleming, like Bree Pasquale, sat next to the table rather than beneath it. Harris shot her with his shotgun, hitting her in the back, killing her instantly. He continued to shoot at the table behind her, hitting Townsend and Kreutz again, and wounding Jeanna Park. An autopsy later revealed that Townsend had been killed by the first shot.

At 11:37 a.m., the shooters moved to the center of the library where they continued to reload their weapons at a table midway across the room. Harris noticed a student nearby, and asked him to identify himself. The student was John Savage, an acquaintance of Klebold's. Savage asked Klebold what they were doing, to which Klebold replied, "Oh, just killing people." Savage asked if they were going to kill him. Klebold said "What?" because the fire alarms were going off. Savage asked again if they were going to kill him. Klebold hesitated, and then told him to leave the library. Savage fled immediately, and escaped via the library's main entrance.

After Savage was gone, Harris turned and fired his carbine at the table directly north of where they had been, hitting Daniel Mauser in the face at close range, killing him. Both shooters moved south from there and fired randomly under another table, critically injuring Jennifer Doyle and Austin Eubanks, and fatally wounding Corey DePooter. DePooter, the last victim of the massacre, was credited with keeping his friends calm during the ordeal. At this point, several witnesses heard Harris and Klebold comment on how they no longer found a thrill in shooting their victims. Klebold was quoted as having said, "Maybe we should start knifing people; that might be more fun." They had each brought two knives in case it came down to hand-to-hand combat ... or to do what Klebold suggested. Both shooters moved away from the table and headed toward the library's main counter. Harris threw a Molotov cocktail toward the southwestern end of the library as he went, but it failed to explode. He came around the east side of the counter and Klebold joined him from the west, converging near where Evan Todd had moved after the copier incident. The shooters made fun of Todd, who was wearing a hat, which meant that he was a jock. When the shooters wanted to see his face, he lifted the hat up partway, so they could not see it. Klebold asked Todd to give him one reason why he should not kill him, and Todd replied, "I don't want trouble." The shooters continued taunting him and debated killing him, but they eventually walked away.

At this point, Harris's nose was bleeding heavily, which is what may have prompted him to decide to leave the library. Klebold turned and fired a shot into an open library staff break room, hitting a small television. He slammed a chair down on top of the computer terminal that was on the library counter, directly above where Patti Nielson had hidden. The two walked out of the library at 11:42 a.m., ending the massacre.

Immediately, thirty-four uninjured and ten injured students, evacuated the library through the north door which led out to the sidewalk adjacent the west entrance, where the rampage had begun. Patrick Ireland, who had been knocked unconscious, and Lisa Kreutz, who was unable to move, remained in the building. Patti Nielson joined Brian Anderson and the three library staff in the exterior break room into which Klebold had earlier fired shots. They locked themselves in and remained there until they were freed at approximately 3:30 p.m.

After leaving the library, the pair went into the science area and threw a small firebomb into an empty storage closet. When the bomb exploded, they ran off while a teacher in the adjacent room put out the fire. They proceeded toward the south hallway, stopped, and shot into an empty science room at the end of the hall.

At approximately 11:44 a.m., they went down the staircase into the cafeteria where they were recorded by the security cameras. The recording shows Harris kneeling on the landing and firing a shot toward a propane bomb, unsuccessfully attempting to detonate it. He took a sip from one of the drinks left behind by fleeing students as Klebold approached the propane bomb. The recording shows Klebold lighting a Molotov cocktail and throwing it at the propane bomb. As the two left the cafeteria, it exploded, partially detonating one of the propane bombs at 11:46 a.m. A gallon of fuel ignited in the same vicinity at 11:48 a.m., causing a fire that was extinguished by the fire sprinklers.

The shooters then left the cafeteria and headed back upstairs. Once again on the upper level, they wandered around the main north and south hallways of the school, shooting aimlessly. They walked through the south hallway, past the social studies section, and into the main office before returning to the north hallway. Several times, they looked through windows on the classroom doors, and even made eye contact with students, but never attempted to enter the rooms. After leaving the main office, the pair went up to a bathroom entrance and began taunting students inside, saying "We know you're in there," and "Let's kill anyone we find in here," but they never actually entered the bathroom. At 11:55 a.m., the two returned to the cafeteria and entered the kitchen briefly, only to return up the staircase and into the south hallway, at 11:58 a.m. At 12:02 p.m., the shooters re-entered the library, now empty of all living students except for the unconscious Patrick Ireland and Lisa Kreutz. Once inside, they shot at police through the west windows again to no avail. At approximately 12:08 p.m., they moved over to the bookshelves near the table where Patrick Ireland lay. There, they shot themselves.

Patrick Ireland regained and lost consciousness several times, and crawled over to the windows. At 2:38 p.m., he attempted to exit, falling out the library window near two SWAT team members, a scene rebroadcast on many media outlets. As documented by the video footage, the SWAT team members were later criticized for allowing Ireland's body to drop over seven feet to the ground while doing nothing to attempt to catch him or break his fall.

Lisa Kreutz remained injured in the library. In an interview, she recalled hearing somebody say something like, "You in the library..." around the time Eric Harris and Dylan Klebold were getting ready to commit suicide. She lay bleeding in the library until police arrived. Kreutz said that she kept track of time by the school's bells, becoming lightheaded when she tried to move. She was removed, along with Ms. Nielson, Brian Anderson, and the three staff, at 3:22 p.m.

A call for additional ammunition for police officers in case of a shootout came at 12:20 p.m. The killers had ceased shooting just minutes earlier. Authorities reported pipe bombs at 1:00 p.m., and two SWAT teams entered the school at 1:09 p.m., moving from classroom to classroom, discovering hidden students and faculty. All students, teachers, and school employees were taken away, questioned, and then offered medical care in small holding areas before being bussed to meet with family members at Leawood Elementary. Officials found the bodies in the library by 3:30 p.m.

By 4:00 p.m., the sheriff made an initial estimate of twenty-five dead students and teachers. The estimate was ten over the true count, but close to the total count of wounded students. He stated that police officers were searching the bodies of Harris and Klebold. At 4:30 p.m., the school was declared safe. At 5:30 p.m., additional officers were called in, as more explosives were found in the parking lot and on the roof. By 6:15 p.m., officials had found a bomb in Klebold's car in the parking lot. The sheriff decided to mark the entire school as a crime scene. Thirteen of the dead, including the shooters, were still inside the school at the time. At 10:45 p.m., the bomb in the car detonated when an officer tried to defuse it. The car was damaged, but no one was injured. In the end, twelve students and one teacher were killed; twenty-four other students were injured. Three more were injured indirectly as they attempted to escape the school. Harris and Klebold are thought to have committed suicide about forty-five minutes after the massacre began.

Chapter 9: Ecole Polytechnique Massacre

Marc Lépine

Lepine was born Gamil Rodrigue Liass Gharbi on October 26th, 1964, in Montreal, Canada, to Rachid Liass Gharbi, an Algerian-born executive, and Monique Lépine, a Canadian nurse.

His father was abusive and contemptuous of women. After his parents separated when he was seven, his mother returned to nursing to support her children. Lépine and his younger sister lived with other families, seeing their mother on weekends. Lépine was considered bright but withdrawn, and had difficulties with peer and family relationships.

Instability and violence marked the family. They moved frequently, and much of Lépine's early childhood was spent in Costa Rica and Puerto Rico where his father was working for a Swiss mutual funds company. In 1968, the family returned to Montreal permanently, shortly before a stock market crash led to the loss of much of their assets. Gharbi was an authoritarian, possessive, and jealous man, frequently violent towards his wife and his children. He was also neglectful and abusive towards his children, particularly his son, and discouraged any tenderness as he considered it spoiling. In 1970, following an incident in which

Gharbi struck his son so hard that the marks on his face were visible a week later, his mother decided to leave her husband. Their legal separation was finalized in 1971, and the divorce in 1976. Taunted as an Arab because of his name, at the age of fourteen young Gamil Gharbi legally changed it to "Marc Lépine," citing hatred of his father as his reason.

Seeking a good male role model for her son, Lepine's mother arranged for a Big Brother, and for two years the experience proved positive for Lépine as he, often with his best friend, enjoyed the time spent with his Big Brother, learning about photography and motorcycles. Lepine also enjoyed designing and building electronic gadgets, and watching action and horror movies, but developed an interest in World War II, and an admiration of Adolf Hitler. Lépine took considerable responsibility at home, cleaning and doing repairs while his mother worked.

In 1979, the Big Brother meetings ceased abruptly when the Big Brother was detained on suspicion of molesting young boys. Both Lépine and his Big Brother denied that any molestation had occurred. Lepine moved out of his mother's home into his own apartment, and in 1986, applied to study engineering at École Polytechnique de Montréal. He was admitted on the condition that he completed two compulsory courses, including one in solution chemistry.

In 1987, Lépine took a job at a hospital but was fired for aggressive behaviour, disrespect of superiors, and carelessness in his work. He was enraged at his dismissal, and at the time described a plan in which he'd go on a murderous rampage and then commit suicide. His friends noted that he was unpredictable, flying into rages when frustrated.

In April of 1989, he met with a university

admissions officer, and complained about how women were taking over the job market from men. In August of 1989, Lépine picked up an application for a firearms-acquisition certificate, and received his permit in mid-October. On November 21st, 1989, Lépine purchased a Ruger Mini-14 semi-automatic rifle at a local sporting goods store. He told the clerk that he was going to use it to hunt small game.

Sometime after 4 p.m. on December 6th, 1989, Marc Lépine arrived at the building housing the École Polytechnique, an engineering school affiliated with the University of Montréal, armed with a rifle and a hunting knife. Lépine was familiar with the layout of the building as he had been in and around the École Polytechnique at least seven times in the weeks leading up to the event. Lépine sat for a time in the office of the registrar on the second floor. He was seen rummaging through a green plastic bag, and did not speak to anyone, even when a staff member asked if she could help him. He appeared agitated, as if waiting for someone who had failed to arrive. He made eye contact with no one; his posture was stiff and his expression was grim. When an employee in the office asked if he needed assistance, he got up, grabbed his bag without a word, and walked away. The employee did not think much about it. The end of the semester was a tough time for students, and many were tired.

Lepine left the office. The halls had cleared and no one was about, no one who could raise an alarm. People in the offices were preparing to leave for the day. That would work in his favor. This was the moment. He had attached a high-capacity banana clip magazine so he could fire thirty rounds in quick succession, and he had plenty of ammunition. He was ready.

At around 5:10 p.m., he went to the second floor mechanical engineering class of about sixty students. After approaching the student giving a presentation, he said, "Everyone stop everything." Professor Bouchard looked at him, annoyed. He squinted as if trying to remember who this student was. In French, the young man asked the ten female students to get up and move across the room. He then told the men to leave. No one moved. A few people laughed, thinking it some kind of joke. That was the worst thing they could have done. Lepine had considered himself humiliated enough in his twenty-five years. On this day, of all days, he was not going to be treated in that way.

Lifting his rifle, he shot twice into the ceiling. It was no joke. "You're all a bunch of feminists!" he shouted angrily. "And I hate feminists!" One of the students, Nathalie Provost, said, "Look, we are just women studying engineering, not necessarily feminists ready to march on the streets to shout we are against men, just students intent on leading a normal life." Lépine responded that, "You're women, you're going to be engineers." He then opened fire on the students from left to right, killing six, and wounding three others, including Provost, who he shot three times. Before leaving the room, he wrote the word "shit" twice on a student project.

Lépine continued into the second floor corridor and wounded three students before entering another room where he twice attempted to shoot a female student. His weapon failed to fire so he entered the emergency staircase where he was seen reloading his gun. He returned to the room he had just left, but the students had locked the door. Lépine fired three shots into the door, but the door would not open. Moving along the corridor, he shot at others, wounding one, before moving towards the financial services office where he shot and killed a woman through the window of the door she had just locked. He next went down to the first floor cafeteria, where about a hundred people were gathered. The crowd scattered after he shot a woman standing near the kitchen and wounded another student. Entering an unlocked storage area at the end of the cafeteria, Lépine shot and killed two more women hiding there. He told a male and a female student to come out from under a table; they complied and were not shot.

By this time, police had arrived and had assembled outside. Several went to cover the exits, lest the gunman slip away, but it took nearly twenty minutes before they decided to enter. They were not certain where he was and did not wish to endanger anyone. Calls went to a dispatcher for more ambulances, and those wounded students who could walk on their own went to meet them at the roadblocks.

Lépine then walked up an escalator to the third floor where he shot and wounded one female and two male students in the corridor. He entered another classroom and told the three students giving a presentation to "get out," shooting and wounding Maryse Leclair, who was standing on the low platform at the front of the classroom. He fired on students in the front row and then killed two women who were trying to escape the room; other students dove under their desks. Lépine fired towards some of the female students, wounding three of them and killing another.

He changed the magazine in his weapon and moved to the front of the class, shooting in all directions. At this point, the wounded Leclair asked for help. Maryse Leclair was down, but still alive. She pleaded for assistance, which attracted the gunman back to her. Those who survived this bloodbath recounted for newspapers what he did next. The strange young man sat down next to the wounded woman, quietly pulled a knife from the sheath strapped to his body, and used it to stab her in the heart. She screamed in surprise and pain. This violent act shocked those who were watching. The man had no mercy, but there was nothing anyone could do. He pulled the knife out and then plunged it in twice more until the girl laid silent, blood gushing from her wounds.

The gunman said, "Ah, shit." He turned the rifle's barrel toward his own face, pressed the muzzle against his forehead, and pulled the trigger. The rifle exploded, blowing off part of his skull and he fell to the floor. No one moved. The place smelled of hot metal, gunpowder, and fresh blood. Nevertheless, clearly it was over.

About sixty bullets remained in the boxes he carried with him. He had killed fourteen women in total (twelve engineering students, one nursing student, and one employee of the university) and injured fourteen other people, including four men.

As police came in, Montreal Police Director of Public Relations Pierre Leclair entered the building and went from one floor to another to assess the situation. Through a window in the third-floor corridor, he saw a young woman lying on a platform, on her back. He stopped. He could not believe what he was seeing. It was his daughter. Rushing to her, he realized that she was among those who had been killed; more horribly, she had been stabbed as well as shot.

It would take a while to piece together why Lepine had caused so much slaughter, but he had stated enough about his intent for students to tell reporters that his rampage had been anti-feminist. He had wanted to shoot only women.

A three-page letter was found in the pocket of his jacket. The letter was never officially made public, but was leaked in November of 1990 to Francine Pelletier, and published in the newspaper, La Presse. In his suicide letter, Lépine cited political motives, blaming feminists for ruining his life. He considered himself rational and expressed admiration for Denis Lortie, who had mounted an attack on the Quebec National Assembly in 1984 for political reasons, killing three Quebec government employees. The letter also contained a list of nineteen Quebec women whom Lépine apparently wished to kill because of their feminism. Another letter, written to a friend, promised the explanation to the massacre lay by following clues left in Lépine's apartment. The hunt led only to a suitcase of computer games and hardware.

The following is a translation of the suicide letter written by Lépine on the day of the shooting:

"Forgive the mistakes, I had 15 minutes to write this. Would you note that if I commit suicide today 89-12-06 it is not for economic reasons (for I have waited until I exhausted all my financial means, even refusing jobs) but for political reasons. Because I have decided to send the feminists, who have always ruined my life, to their Maker. For seven years life has brought me no joy and being totally blasé, I have decided to put an end to those viragos. I tried in my youth to enter the Forces as an officer cadet, which would have allowed me possibly to get into the arsenal and precede Lortie in a raid. They refused me because antisocial (sic). I therefore had to wait until this day to execute my plans. In between, I continued my studies in a haphazard way for they never really interested

me, knowing in advance my fate. Which did not prevent me from obtaining very good marks despite my theory of not handing in work and the lack of studying before exams. Even if the Mad Killer epithet will be attributed to me by the media, I consider myself a rational erudite that only the arrival of the Grim Reaper has forced to take extreme acts. For why persevere to exist if it is only to please the government. Being rather backward-looking by nature (except for science), the feminists have always enraged me. They want to keep the advantages of women (e.g. cheaper insurance, extended maternity leave preceded by a preventative leave, etc.) while seizing for themselves those of men. Thus it is an obvious truth that if the Olympic Games removed the Men-Women distinction, there would be Women only in the graceful events. So the feminists are not fighting to remove that barrier. They are so opportunistic they [do not]

---

neglect to profit from the knowledge accumulated by men through the ages. They always try to misrepresent them every time they can. Thus, the other day, I heard they were honoring the Canadian men and women who fought at the frontline during the world wars. How can you explain that since women were not authorized to go to the frontline??? Will we hear of Caesar's female legions and female galley slaves who of course took up 50% of the ranks of history, though they never existed. A real Casus Belli. Sorry for this too brief letter." Marc Lépine

Chapter 10: Red Lake High Massacre

Jeff Weise

Jeffrey James Weise was born on August 8th, 1988 in Minneapolis, Minnesota, the only child to Daryl Allen Lussier, Jr. and Joanne Elizabeth Weise. His mother was alleged to be a violent alcoholic who would physically and emotionally abuse her first-born son. Shortly thereafter, in

137

1992, Joanne Weise began dating a Lakota man named Timothy Troy DesJarlait. The two married on June 27th, 1998, and divorced in February, 2000.

On July 21st, 1997, Daryl Lussier, Jr. committed suicide via shotgun wound to the head, after a two-day standoff with the Red Lake Police Department in Red Lake. On March 5th, 1999, Joanne Weise suffered severe brain damage when a tractor-trailer crashed into her car on a highway in Minneapolis. She and her cousin Elizabeth May Jourdain, were drinking alcohol and driving. Jourdain's was killed and Joanne had to be committed to a nursing home in Bloomington, Minnesota. Consequently, Jeff was placed in the care of his paternal grandmother, Shelda Lussier in Red Lake. He expressed frustration with living in Red Lake, and believed that his life was beyond his control.

Weise's depression prompted a suicide attempt in May of 2004. Describing his experience in a post made on the website Above Top Secret, he said:

"I had went through a lot of things in my life that had driven me to a darker path than most choose to take. I split the flesh on my wrist with a box opener, painting the floor of my bedroom with blood I shouldn't have spilt. After sitting there for what seemed like hours (which apparently was only minutes), I had the revelation that this was not the path. It was my division (sic) to seek medical treatment, as on the other hand I could have chosen to sit there until enough blood drained from my downward lacerations on my wrists to die."

Jeffrey was hospitalized in Thief River Falls due to suicidal thoughts. He was hospitalized for 72 hours.

At noon, Weise retrieved a .22 caliber pistol from his bedroom and fatally shot his paternal grandfather, Daryl Lussier, Sr., who was a Sergeant with the Red Lake Police Department, two times in the head and ten times in the chest as he was sleeping. It is not known how Weise obtained the pistol, but, according to his friends, he may have had it in his possession for as long as one year. Weise then stole Lussier's two police-issue weapons, a .40 caliber Glock 23 pistol, and a Remington 12 gauge pump-action shotgun. He then fatally shot Michelle Leigh Sigana, Lussier's girlfriend, two times in the head, as she was carrying laundry up the stairs.

Weise then drove his grandfather's squad car to Red Lake Senior High School in Red Lake, arriving at around 2:45 p.m. As he entered the school through the main entrance, he encountered two unarmed security guards who were operating a metal detector. Weise shot and killed security guard Derrick Brun while the other security guard managed to escape without injury. Weise then proceeded through the main corridor of the school and began shooting into an English classroom, killing three students and one teacher, and wounding three students.

Jeffrey May, a sixteen-year-old sophomore, attempted to wrestle Weise inside the classroom, and managed to stab him in the stomach with a pencil. This allowed students to evacuate the classroom to safety. Weise retaliated, however, by shooting May two times in the neck and one time in the jaw, leaving him injured, but alive. May managed to survive the ordeal. Another student, Chase Lussier, was rumored to have jumped in the line of a shotgun blast to save another student.

Witnesses say Weise smiled as he was shooting at people. One witness said that he asked a student if he believed in God, a link commonly believed to be reminiscent of the events that took place during the Columbine High School massacre. At around 2:52 p.m., Weise returned to the main entrance where he killed two students and wounded two others.

FBI special agent Paul McCabe stated Weise engaged in a shoot-out with the police that lasted for about four minutes. Eventually Weise retreated to a vacant classroom after sustaining one gunshot wound to the abdomen and one to the right arm. None of the officers were injured. Weise, lay against a wall in the classroom, put the shotgun barrel in his mouth, and fired, instantly killing himself.

Chapter 11: Beslan School Hostage

Riyadus Saliheen

Initially, the identity of the attackers was not immediately clear. It was widely assumed that they were separatists from nearby Chechnya. The Russian government had stated that the attackers were an international group consisting of some Arabs and even one local resident. There were thirty-two attackers, five of whom were women, who made the following demands:

- Withdrawal of Russian troops from Chechnya.

- The Presence of the following people in the school:

- Aleksander Dzasokhov, President of North Ossetia

- Murat Ziazikov, President of Ingushetia,

- Alu Alkhanov, President of Chechnya

- Aslambek Aslakhanov, or Mukharbek Aushev

- Vladimir Rushailo, Executive Secretary for the Commonwealth of Independent States.

The Crisis – Day 1

Every year in every school in the Russian Federation, on the first day of September, citizens celebrate a holiday known as the "Day of Knowledge" at school. The children are commonly accompanied by their parents and other family members dressed in their finest clothes. After listening to introductions and speeches from the staff and students, the 'First Graders' give a flower to the 'Last Graders.' The Last Graders then take the First Graders to their first class. In 2004, on September 1st at School Number One in Beslan, this tradition was deliberately used by terrorists as an opportunity to seize the school and take hostages. The result was hundreds of children and entire families wounded or killed. At about 9:40 a.m., a group of thirty-two men and women stormed Beslan's Middle School Number One, whose pupils ranged from seven to eighteen years old. Most of the attackers wore black ski masks and a few were seen carrying explosive belts. After an exchange of gunfire with police in which five officers and one perpetrator were killed, the attackers seized the school building, taking more than 1,300 hostages.

This number was confirmed by teachers later. Many hostages were schoolchildren under the age of eighteen. There were also many parents and staff inside. About fifty people managed to flee to safety in the initial attack and alert authorities. Repeated shooting was later heard coming from the school buildings, thought by some to be for the intimidation of security forces. It was later revealed that the attackers had killed twenty adult- male hostages and had thrown their bodies out of the building. The attackers were also outraged by the authorities undercounting the number of hostages. The attackers moved the hostages to the school gymnasium on the first day, mined the gym and the rest of the building with improvised explosive devices, and surrounded it with tripwires. In a further bid to deter rescue attempts, they threatened to kill fifty hostages for every one of their own members killed by the police, and twenty hostages for every gunman injured.

They also threatened to blow up the school should government forces attack. The Russian government initially said that it would not use force to rescue the hostages, and negotiations towards a peaceful resolution did take place on the first and second days, led by Leonid Roshal, a pediatrician for whom the hostage-takers had reportedly asked for by name. Roshal had helped negotiate the release of children in the 2002 Moscow Theatre Siege. At Russia's request, a special meeting of the United Nations Security Council was convened on the evening of September 1st. The council members demanded "the immediate and unconditional release of all hostages of the terrorist attack." U.S. President George W. Bush reportedly offered "support in any form" to Russia in dealing with the crisis.

Day 2

On September 2nd, 2004, negotiations between Roshal and the hostage-takers proved unsuccessful, and they refused to accept food, water, and medicines for the hostages, or even for the bodies of the dead to be removed from the school. Many hostages, especially children, took off their shirts and other articles of clothing because of the sweltering heat, which led to rumors of sexual assault, though the hostages later explained it was merely to keep cool.

In the afternoon, following their negotiations with former Ingush President Ruslan Aushev, the gunmen agreed to release twenty-six nursing women and their infants. One infant was handed to Aushev as its mother refused to leave the school while her other children remained inside. At around 3:30 p.m., two explosions occurred at the school, approximately ten minutes apart from one another. These were later revealed to be the explosions of rocket-propelled grenades, fired by the hostage-takers in an apparent attempt to keep the security forces well away from the school.

Day 3

On the afternoon of September 3rd, 2004, the hostage-takers agreed to allow medical workers to remove bodies from the school grounds. The removal team, reportedly consisting of FSB (Federal Security Service, formerly known as the KGB) officers, began to approach the school at 1:04 p.m., but the hostage-takers opened fire, and two large explosions were heard.

Two of the medical workers died; the rest fled under a hail of gunfire. Part of the gymnasium also collapsed, allowing a group of about thirty hostages to escape, but they were fired on by the gunmen, and then caught in crossfire as the

Russian army and armed civilians tried to fire at the terrorists. Many of the escapees were killed. Ruslan Aushev, the negotiator during the siege, told the Novaya Gazeta that the initial explosion was set off by a hostage-taker accidentally tripping over a wire. As a result, armed civilians, some of them apparently fathers of the hostages, started shooting. Reportedly, no security forces or hostage-takers were shooting at this point, but the gunfire led the hostage-takers to believe that the school was being stormed. In response, they set off their bombs. It was at this point that Russian Special Forces activated their action plan to storm the school to rescue any possible survivors. A disorganized battle broke out as the Special Forces sought to enter the school and cover the escape of the hostages. Some panicking Russian army recruits fled the scene while the Special Forces commandos blew holes in walls to allow hostages to escape. A massive level of force was used. The special forces, regular army, and Interior Ministry troops were all involved, as were helicopter gunships and at least one tank. Many local civilians also joined in the battle, having brought along their own weapons.

Afterwards, the Russian government defended the use of tanks and other heavy weaponry, arguing that it was used after surviving hostages escaped from the school; however, this contradicts eyewitness accounts and common sense, as many hostages were seriously wounded and could not possibly escape by themselves.

The attack was followed by large explosions of other detonating bombs and several Shmel fuel-air explosive rockets used by the government forces, which destroyed the gym and set much of the building on fire. By 3:00

p.m., two hours after the assault began, Russian troops claimed control of most of the school. Fighting, however, continued as evening fell, and three gunmen held up in the basement with a number of hostages. They, and the hostages they were holding, were eventually killed. During the battle, a group of hostage-takers, approximately thirteen of them, broke through the military cordon and took refuge nearby. Two of those thirteen were reportedly women who allegedly attempted to blend into the crowd and escape disguised as medical personnel. The military cordon had been compromised as they'd permitted the passage of hostage's relatives, dressed in civilian clothing and, in some cases, bearing firearms. A few of the escapees were said to be cornered in a residential two-story house within 120 feet of the gym. Whether or not they had hostages was unknown. The house was destroyed using tanks and flamethrowers by

11:00 p.m., on September the third.

In the aftermath, Deputy Prosecutor General Alexander Fridinsky believed that thirty-one of the thirty-two attackers had been confirmed dead, and one had been captured. One suspected hostage-taker was beaten to death by the fathers of hostages when he was injured and being driven to the hospital. Another suspected terrorist was assassinated on the scene, an event filmed by the Sky News crew. According to the official data, 331 civilians and eleven commandos died. At least one surviving female hostage committed suicide after returning home. Many other survivors remained in severe shock. Some injured survivors died in hospitals.

The Russian government has been heavily criticized by many locals who, days after the end of the siege, did not know whether their children were living or dead. Human remains were even found in the nearby garbage dump several months later, prompting further outrage.

During the operation, eleven Russian Soldiers of the special groups Alpha and Vympel were killed, among them the commander of Alpha. This was the highest casualty rate ever suffered in a single engagement in the history of these units. One of their members said they'd rescued children first, and the hostage-takers had then shot at their backs; that was why they'd suffered such high losses (another commando admitted shooting children used by the terrorists as human shields). In addition, many were accidentally hit by civilian militiamen, who either fired indiscriminately or mistook them for the hostage takers. Wounds of varying severity were received by more than thirty fighters of the OSNAZ Special Forces. In May, 2005, the only known accused terrorist to survive the Beslan massacre was Nur-Pashi Kulayev. All local lawyers refused to defend Kulayev. Albert Pliyev was appointed, reluctantly, as his lawyer. The local people at the time wanted to either lynch the defendant or sentence him to the death penalty. Over 1,340 people act as the injured party on the trial. Kulayev was charged with murder, terrorism, kidnapping, and other crimes, and pled guilty on seven of the counts. Kulayev is said to be incarcerated in a high-security prison on the small lake island of Ognenny Ostrov in the Vologda region.

In May of 2002, the Secret Service published a report that examined thirty-seven school shootings in the United States. They published the following findings:

- Incidents of targeted violence at schools were rarely sudden, impulsive acts.

- Prior to most incidents, other people knew about the attacker's idea and/or plan to attack.

- Most attackers did not threaten their targets directly prior to advancing the attack.

- There is no accurate or useful profile of students who engaged in targeted school violence.

- Most attackers engaged in behavior prior to the incident that caused others concern, or indicated a need for help.

- Most attackers had difficulty coping with significant losses or personal failures.

- Many attackers had considered or attempted suicide.

- Many attackers felt bullied, persecuted, or injured by others prior to the attack.

- Most attackers had access to, and had used

weapons, prior to the attack.

- In many cases, other students were involved in some capacity.

- Despite prompt law enforcement responses, most shooting incidents were stopped by means other than law enforcement intervention.

Chapter 12: Going Postal

According to the Federal Bureau of Investigation (FBI) the general definition of a spree murder is two or more murders committed by an offender, or offenders, without a cooling-off period – the lack of a cooling-off period marking the difference between a spree murder and a serial murder. Serial killers are different in that the murders are clearly separate events, happening at different times, while the attacks of mass murderers are defined by one incident, with no distinctive time period between the murders.

Another common term for spree killings is 'going postal,' meaning becoming extremely and uncontrollably angry, often to the point of violence, and usually in a workplace environment. The expression derives from a series of incidents from 1983 onward in which United States Postal Service (USPS) workers shot and killed managers, fellow workers, and members of the police or general public in acts of mass murder. Between 1986 and 1997, more than forty people were gunned down by spree killers in at least twenty incidents of workplace rage.

Chapter 13: Michigan Massacre

Rodrick Dantzler

In Grand Rapids, Michigan, on July 7th, 2011, seven people were killed and others injured by Rodrick Shonte Dantzler, thirty-four, a building technician. His victims included his estranged wife, their children, other innocent people, and his former girlfriend. Dantzler had a rather shady childhood. In 1992, at the age of fifteen, he was convicted for burglary as a juvenile. He was raised by his stepfather who abused drugs, and his mother, but she kicked him out of her house when he was eighteen, allegedly over threats he repeatedly made. His mother would later say that he had an explosive temper and acted violently with thinking. After being kicked out of his mother's home, he set fire to her house, and in 1997 was convicted of destroying property and domestic violence. From 2000 to 2005, he served time in prison for a road rage shooting incident. During his time incarcerated, he obtained his high school diploma and partook in anger management programs.

Upon his release from prison, Dantzler was said to be under doctor's care, taking prescribed medication for bipolar disorder, and receiving a disability pension. In 2010 he was sent back to prison for another year after being convicted of assault and battery.

Just days before the shooting spree, Dantzler took his daughter and wife to Michigan's Adventure in Muskegon. His wife, Jennifer Heeren, was planning on separating from him, but it is not known whether Dantzler was aware of it or not. It is known that on the day of the shootings, he drank a lot of alcohol and used cocaine.

The murdering began in the house of Dantzler's former girlfriend, Amanda Emkens. There, he killed Emkens, her sister, Kimberlee, and her sister's ten year old daughter, Marisa. He then went home where his wife, their daughter, and his wife's parents lived, and killed all of them too.

Dantzler called his mother and told her what he had done. His mother, in turn, contacted the police, who dispatched units and subsequently discovered the bodies. The police closed down the area and told neighbors to remain inside their homes, as they didn't know at this time where the killer was located. At this point, Dantzler was near Godfrey Avenue, where he shot and injured a man in an apparent road rage incident before abandoning his Town Car and taking a Suburban from another person – who luckily jumped out of the vehicle. At 7:00 pm, April Swanson, a friend of Dantzler, called police on her cell phone to report that Dantzler was following her in a Suburban. He shot her from his vehicle at Fulton Street and Division Avenue. She suffered a serious but non-life-threatening arm injury. Police intervened by ramming Dantzler's vehicle. They exchanged gunfire, but no officers were shot. The suspect was chased by police who attempted to disable his vehicle as he drove through downtown Grand Rapids. Dantzler turned onto eastbound Interstate 96, where he crossed the median and continued eastward in the westbound lanes against the flow of traffic, and crashed into a freeway ditch around 7:15 pm.

Dantzler ran from his vehicle and entered the residence of Joyce Bean on Rickman Avenue. He held her, her boyfriend Steve Helderman, and Meg Holmes hostage. At 9:30 pm, after receiving Gatorade and cigarettes from police, he released Ms. Bean. Two more hours of negotiations ensued with police, then Dantzler released the other two hostages and shot himself in the head. It is believed by police that Dantzler was hunting his former girlfriends in retaliation for his wife leaving him.

Chapter 14: Geneva County Massacre

Michael McLendon

In Kinston, Geneva and Samson, Alabama, on March 10th, 2009, Michael Kenneth McLendon, twenty-eight, killed ten people, literally wiping out his whole family.

By all accounts McLendon had a normal childhood. He was quiet, likeable, a straight 'A' student in school, never got into trouble, and was close to his family. He was also, however, a failed Marine and auxiliary policeman who had lost his job, and he had become embroiled in a bitter dispute over a family Bible in the weeks leading up to the killing spree. The shooting spree began in Kinston, Alabama, when he shot his mother in the head, placed blankets soaked in gasoline over her, and set the house on fire. Before leaving, he shot his mother's three dogs and arranged them at her feet. He then went to a relative's home in Samson where he shot several family members, and a neighbor and her daughter. The neighbor was the wife of a Sheriff's Deputy.

Mclendon then killed a pedestrian along the side of the road before stopping at a gas station where he killed a random customer. From there, he headed towards Geneva along Highway 52, and killed another man who attempted to subdue him. McLendon was chased by police and he shot at several cars during the pursuit. Arriving at a Geneva metal products plant where he used to work, he got into a shootout with the police. Several people were injured, including Police Chief Frankie Lindsey, who was shot in the arm. McLendon eventually shot himself in the head and died instantly.

Detectives later discovered a hit list in his home targeting several corporations, and a letter confessing that he meant to murder his mother and then commit suicide. The letter mentioned a disagreement over a legal issue with his family.

One day after this massacre, a school shooting causing fifteen deaths took place in Winnenden, Germany. Whether the massacre in Geneva County was an actuator for the Winnenden killing could not be determined.

Chapter 15: Winnenden School Shooting

Tim Kretschmer

The day after the Geneva Massacre in Alabama, another school shooting took place in Winnenden, Germany. Tim Kretschmer, seventeen, killed sixteen and injured another eleven people at the Albertville School on March 11th, 2009.

Kretschmer did not have a criminal record,

but in 2008 received treatment as an inpatient at the Weissenhoff Psychiatric Clinic near the town of Heilbronn. After being discharged, he was supposed to continue his treatment as an outpatient, but did not follow through. According to a psychiatric report prepared for the prosecutor's office, Kretschmer met five times with a therapist and talked about his growing anger and violent urges; the therapist then informed Kretschmer's parents.

Kretschmer was described by a friend as a lonely and frustrated person who felt rejected by society. Another friend described him as a quiet student who began to withdraw from his peers. Media reports said that he enjoyed playing the video game, Counter Strike, and playing with air soft guns. He also shot his guns in the forest behind his home and in the basement of his house. After the shooting spree, inspecting his computer, officers found that he was interested in sadomasochistic scenes where men are bound and humiliated by women. He viewed such a movie the evening before the crime.

Just hours prior to commencing his killing spree, Tim Kretschmer posted the following message on the internet: "I've had enough. I'm fed up with this bloody life. It's always the same thing, everyone laughs at me, and no one recognizes my potential. I mean this seriously – I've got a weapon here and tomorrow morning I'm going to go to my old school and give them hell. Maybe I'll escape and you will hear from me tomorrow morning."

After stealing a 9mm Beretta semi-automatic from his parent's bedroom, Kretschmer went to the Albertville-Realschule at about 9:30am. He ran quickly to the top floor classrooms and chemistry laboratory and started shooting students. Most were females, and shot in the head. He fired a total of sixty rounds in those classrooms.

The school's principal immediately broadcasted a coded announcement, "Mrs. Koma is coming," which is 'amok' spelled in reverse. This code was introduced in all German schools after the Erfurt School Massacres in April of 2002. It alerts teachers to lock their classroom doors. Just minutes later, the police were notified by several students who called emergency services from their cell phones. Three officers arrived at 9:33 am, interrupting the killing spree. Kretschmer, however, shot at the officers, and killed two female teachers in the hallway as he was running out of the building, where he shot and killed a janitor in the parking lot.

A huge number of police officers secured the school and searched for Kretschmer all over

Winnenden for hours without success. In the meantime, at about 10 a.m., Kretschmer carjacked a Volkswagen at a car park. From the rear seat, he ordered the driver, Igor Wolf, to drive towards Wendlingen, approximately twenty-five miles away. Igor Wolf later reported that when he asked Kretschmer why he was carjacking him, Kretschmer replied, "For fun, because it is fun." The gunman reloaded his magazines and inquired about finding another school. At about noon, when Mr. Wolf saw an approaching police car at the highway, he steered the car towards a grassy median and jumped out.

Kretschmer also left the car and ran into a Volkswagen dealership showroom where he demanded a key for a car. He shot and killed a salesperson and a customer before police descended upon him. The first officer on the scene fired eight shots initially, hitting

Kretschmer in both legs. Kretschmer returned to the showcase, fired at the police, and then ran out the back door to a business complex. While doing so, he injured two officers situated in an unmarked car.

According to witnesses, Kretschmer was firing at random. He then reloaded his gun and shot himself in the head. This last part was captured by on a cell phone video. In total, he fired off 112 rounds of ammunition.

In the aftermath following this horrific crime, Police indicted Tim Kretschmer's father on charges of negligent homicide for not having the 9mm Beretta safely stored. Another fourteen weapons were found in the house, all of them locked up in a gun safe. All of his guns were confiscated.

On February 10th, 2011, the state court found the father guilty of involuntary manslaughter in fifteen cases of bodily harm caused by negligence, and the negligent abandonment of a weapon. He received a suspended sentence of one year and nine months, but has since appealed the verdict.

The families of five of the victims wrote an open letter to Chancellor Angela Merkel, President Horst Köhler, Minister Baden-Württemberg, and President Günther Oettinger, with demands for consequences. They called to prohibit youth from accessing guns in gun clubs, less violence on TV, and a cessation of violent video games. They also called for the reporting of these incidents to be toned down with relation to highlighting details of their crimes, so as to minimize the chance of copycats.

Chapter 16: Fort Hood Shooting Spree

Nidal Malik Hasan

On November 5th, 2009, U.S. Army Major Nidal Malik Hasan shot and killed thirteen and wounding another twenty-nine on the most populous U.S. military base in the world, Fort Hood, Killeen, Texas.

Born in Arlington, Virginia, to Muslim-Palestinian parents, Hasan immediately joined the United States army after graduating high school and spent eight years in the service while earning a bachelor's degree at Virginia Tech in Biochemistry. He went on to earn his Medical degree in 2003, and completed his residency in Psychiatry at the Walter Reed Army Medical Center. He was promoted from captain to major in May of 2009 after completing a fellowship in Disaster and Preventive Psychiatry at the Center of Traumatic Stress. Before being transferred to Fort Hood in July of 2009, however, he received a meager performance evaluation.

It was later understood, post killing-spree, that Hasan was greatly influenced by the killing of two recruiters in Little Rock, Arkansas, by Abdulhakim Mujahid Muhammad. Hasan made peculiar statements against the American military presence in Iraq and Afghanistan, stating that "the Muslims should stand up and fight against the aggressor," referring to the US.

While he had expressed optimism that President Barack Obama would end both wars, he became increasingly agitated and frequently argued with soldiers. Hasan seemed happy about the shooting in Little Rock, but didn't like how the suspect was treated as a criminal. Hasan made statements saying that the U.S. army should get out of Iraq and Afghanistan, and said that more people like Muhammad should "strap bombs on themselves and go into Times Square."

Hasan was scheduled to be deployed to Afghanistan on November 28th. Preceding the shooting spree, Hasan told a local store owner that he was stressed about his forthcoming deployment as he might have to fight and kill fellow Muslims.

In the Soldier Readiness Center at Fort Hood on November 5th, 2009, Hasan shouted 'Allahu Akbar,' meaning 'God is greatest,' and then opened fire, killing thirteen and injuring another twenty-nine. It was the worst shooting ever on an American Military Base, even though the incident, from start to finish, lasted just ten minutes.

As Hasan was running out of the building he exchanged shots with Sergeant Kimberly Munley who he hit twice in the legs. Civilian Police Officer Sergeant Mark Todd also fired on the gunman, hitting him in the spine, subsequently paralyzing him from the waist down. Once down, Officer Todd approached Hasan and kicked his gun away before placing handcuffs on him.

Hasan was formally charged with thirteen counts of premeditated murder and thirty-two counts of attempted murder. Military prosecutors sought the death penalty, but Hasan's lawyer, however, said it was likely that he would plead not guilty by reason of insanity.

The hearing started on October 14th, 2010 with witness testimonies from soldiers who had survived the shootings. On November 15th, the military hearing ended when Hasan's lawyer declined to offer a defense case on the grounds that the White House and Defense Department refused to hand over requested documents pertaining to an intelligence review of the shootings. Neither the defense nor prosecution offered to deliver a closing argument. On November 18th, Colonel James L. Pohl, who served as the investigating officer for the Article 32 hearing, recommended that Hasan be court-martialed and face the death penalty. His recommendation was forwarded to another U.S. Army colonel at Fort Hood who, after filing his own report, presented his recommendation to the post commander. The post commander made the final decision on whether Hasan faced a trial and the death penalty.

On July 6th, 2011, the Fort Hood post commander referred the case to a general court-martial for trial. The court-martial was authorized to consider death as an authorized punishment. On July 27th, 2011, Fort Hood Chief Circuit Judge Colonel Gregory Gross set a March 5th, 2012, trial date for Hasan's court martial. Hasan declined to enter any plea and Judge Gross granted a request by Hasan's attorneys to defer the plea to an unspecified date. Hasan subsequently notified Gross that he had released the civilian attorney who had been his counsel in his previous court appearances. At his court martial, Hasan will instead be represented by three military lawyers at no cost to him. Hasan continues to receive paychecks and medical treatment from the military.

Chapter 17: Standard Gravure

Joseph T. Wesbecker

At the Standard Gravure Plant in Louisville, Kentucky, on September 14th, 1989, eight people were killed and another twelve injured by Joseph Wesbecker, forty-seven, before he committed suicide. Wesbecker was only thirteen months old when his father died, leaving his sixteen year old mother to raise him on her own He was not a very intelligent student in high school and dropped out in the ninth grade; later he obtained his G.E.D. He married, had two sons, and in 1971 moved his family to Kentucky where he worked at a printing plant. In 1978, however, his personal life took a downward turn. His wife left him, they had a custody battle of their children, and Wesbecker admitted himself to a hospital for psychiatric treatment. In 1983 he married again, but it didn't last long and soon he became separated from his family, withdrawn, and living a lonely life off work on disability for his mental illness.

Wesbecker had a long history of psychiatric illness and was treated in hospitals at least three times between 1978 and 1987. He was diagnosed as suffering from alternating episodes of deep depression and manic depression. He was plagued by confusion, anger, and anxiety, and made several attempts to commit suicide. Hospital records suggested that Wesbecker posed a threat to himself and others.

In the years prior to the shooting, Wesbecker more than once threatened to "kill a bunch of people" or to bomb Standard Gravure; at one point he considered hiring an assassin to kill several executives of the company. Apparently he'd even discussed these things with his wife before their divorce. When Wesbecker left Standard Gravure in August of 1988, he told other workers that he would come back, wipe out the place, and get even with the company. Shortly before the shooting, he told one of his aunts that he was upset about things at work, and told her that they'd get their payback. These were things he said all the time, however, and she didn't take the threat too seriously.

At 8:30 a.m., on September 14th, 1989, Wesbecker parked his car in front of the main entrance to the Standard Gravure Plant where he used to work. Before entering the building, he took the following weapons from his car: a SIG Sauer 9mm semi-automatic handgun, a .38 caliber Smith & Wesson Revolver, a bayonet, an AK-47 assault rifle, two MAC-11 submachine guns, and hundreds of rounds of ammunition in a duffel bag.

Taking the elevator to the executive reception area on the third floor, as soon as the doors opened, he began firing at receptionists Sharon Needy and Angela Bowman. Needy was killed, and Bowman paralyzed by a shot in the back. Searching for Michael Shea, president of Standard Gravure, and other supervisors and bosses of the plant, Wesbecker calmly walked through the hallways, deliberately shooting at people. He killed James Husband and injured Forrest Conrad, Paula Warman, and John Stein, a maintenance supervisor, who he shot in the head and abdomen, before heading down the stairs to the pressroom, where he killed Paul Sallee. He then wounded two electricians from Marine Electric that were working on a broken machine, Stanley Hatfield and David Sadenfaden, and left the duffel bag under a stairwell. Wesbecker walked down to the basement where he encountered pressman, John Tingle, who, alerted by the loud noises, wanted to see what was happening. Tingle greeted his colleague, and asked him what was going on. Wesbecker replied, "Hi John...I told them I'd be back. Get away from me." Wesbecker continued his path through the basement, shooting Richard Barger in the back, killing him. According to witnesses, Wesbecker approached Barger's body and apologized; apparently he'd killed him accidentally as he didn't see at whom he was shooting. Back on the press floor, he shot at anyone in his way, killing James Wible and Lloyd White, and finally entered the break room where he emptied his magazine, hitting all seven workers present, killing William Ganote with a shot to the head. Wesbecker then reloaded and resumed firing, fatally wounding Kenneth Fentress. When Wesbecker stepped out to the pressroom, he pulled his SIG Sauer, put it under his chin and shot himself, ending his shooting spree that had lasted for about half an hour. He'd fired about forty rounds of ammunition, and left eight people dead and twelve wounded. Additionally, one person suffered a heart attack.

When police searched Wesbecker's house, they recovered a shotgun, a Colt 9-millimeter revolver, a .32 revolver, and a starter's pistol. They found Wesbecker's will, as well as a copy of Time Magazine on the kitchen table featuring an article about Patrick Purdy who had killed five children and injured thirty others with a Type 56 assault rifle, the same weapon as used by Wesbecker, at a school in Stockton, California, earlier the same year.

Chapter 18: Luby's Massacre

George Hennard

George Hennerd was once referred to as a nice young boy with long hair. He used to be in a band; he was cool and likeable. All that appeared to change one day when he and his father had a vicious altercation that he would never talk about. After that, Hennard changed into a very cold hearted and mainly vicious person. He would regularly fight with other people and shout obscenities. He was always irritated and very reserved. He had a female neighbor with two daughters that he would stalk, going everywhere they went, and he often wrote letters to the girls. When the girls' mother went to the police, she was told that they could not do anything about it because he hadn't committed any crime.

On October 16th, 1991, in Killeen, Texas, Hennard drove his 1987 Ford Ranger pickup truck through the front window of a Luby's Cafeteria in Killeen, Texas, and yelled, "This is what Bell County has done to me!" He then opened fire on patrons and employees with a Glock 17 pistol and later a Ruger P89. He walked around, shooting; about eighty people were in the restaurant at the time.

Thinking that the driver had accidently crashed into the building, Dr. Michael Griffith ran to the driver's side of the pickup truck to offer assistance and was shot instantly. During the shooting, Hennard approached Dr. Suzanna Hupp and her parents, who happened to have a handgun in her vehicle? Her father charged at the gunman in an attempt to restrain him but was gunned down. A short time later her mother was shot and killed also. Another patron, Tommy Vaughn, threw himself through a plate-glass window to allow others to get away. Hennard allowed a woman and her four year old child to leave. He reloaded his guns several times, and still had ammunition remaining when he ended his own life after being cornered and wounded by police. But by then he'd killed twenty-three people while wounding another twenty.

In the aftermath, in 1995 the Texas Legislature passed a shall-issue gun law which requires that all qualifying applicants be issued a Concealed Handgun License, removing the personal good judgment of the issuing authority to deny such licenses. To qualify for a license, one must be free and clear of crimes, attend a minimum of ten hours of classes taught by a state certified instructor, pass a fifty question test, show proficiency in a fifty round shooting test, and pass two background tests, one shallow and one deep.

The proposal to change the law was campaigned by Dr. Suzanna Hupp who had been present at the massacre where both of her parents were shot and killed. She later expressed regret for obeying the law by leaving her firearm in her car rather than keeping it on her person, thinking at the time that it could mean losing her chiropractic license. She testified across the country in support of concealed handgun laws, and was elected to the Texas House of Representatives in 1996. The law was signed by then Governor George W. Bush.

Authors Note: I really admire Dr. Hupp and her efforts of getting this law passed.

Chapter 19: The Walk of Death

Howard Barton Unruh

September 6th, 1949, in Camden, New Jersey, Howard Barton Unruh, twenty-eight, killed thirteen innocent people.

Unruh was the son of Freda and Samuel Unruh, and had a younger brother James. He graduated Woodrow Wilson High School in 1939, enlisted in the U.S. Army, and was sent overseas to fight during World War II. During the war, he was purportedly a heroic tank soldier who served in the Battle of the Bulge and kept scrupulous notes of every German killed, down to details of the corpse. He was honorably discharged in 1945 and returned home with an assortment of medals and firearms. He decorated his bedroom with military items and set up a target range in his basement. His mother supported him by working at a factory while Howard hung around the house and attended daily church services. He briefly attended a pharmacy course at Temple University in Philadelphia but dropped out after only three months.

Unruh had difficulty getting along with his neighbors, and his relations with them worsened in the three months previous to his killing spree. Considered a mama's boy, Unruh was the subject of teasing, and often harassed by neighborhood teens who thought he was homosexual. He was reported to have been unhappy about having had homosexual liaisons in a Philadelphia movie theater. He had only one brief association with a girl prior to his arrest. Ultimately, Unruh became obsessed with his neighbors and started to keep a diary detailing everything he thought was said about him. Next to some of the names was the word, 'retaliate.' He arrived home from a movie theater at 3 am on September 6th to discover that the gate he had just built in front of his house had been stolen. This appears to have been what set him off. Unruh later told the Police, "When I came home last night and found my gate had been stolen, I decided to kill them all."   After sleeping until 8 am, he got up, dressed in his best suit, and ate breakfast with his mother. At some point, he threatened his mother with a wrench, and she left for a friend's home. At 9:20 am, Unruh left the house equipped with a

German Luger handgun, seeking his first victims. In only twelve minutes he shot and killed thirteen people with fourteen shots and injured several others. Although, in general, the killing was premeditated, the victims seemed to be chosen haphazardly. Unruh's first shot missed its planned victim, a bakery truck driver, but then he shot two of five people in a barber shop, sparing the other three that were in the shop. One victim was killed when he happened to block the door to a pharmacy. A motorist was killed when his car slowed to view the body of a victim. Intending to kill a local tailor, Unruh entered his shop, but the tailor was not there; Unruh killed the man's wife instead.

When he heard the sound of sirens from the approaching police, Unruh returned to his apartment and initiated in a standoff. Over sixty police personnel surrounded Unruh's home and a shootout developed. During the blockade, Philip

W. Buxton, a reporter from the Camden Evening Courier, phoned Unruh's home and spoke to him for a short time. On a gut feeling, Buxton had looked up Unruh's number in the phone book. Buxton later recounted the conversation, which was cut short when police hurled tear gas into the apartment:

"What are they doing to you?"

"They haven't done anything to me yet, but I'm doing plenty to them."

"How many have you killed?"

"I don't know yet. I haven't counted them. But it looks like a pretty good score."

"Why are you killing people?"

"I don't know. I can't answer that yet. I'm too busy. I'll have to talk to you later. A couple of friends are coming to get me."

Just minutes after that conversation, Unruh was arrested by the police and taken for interrogation. He told the police that he had spent the previous evening sitting through three showings of a double feature: The Lady Gambles, and I Cheated the Law, stating that he'd thought that actress Barbara Stanwyck was one of his hated neighbors. He provided a careful description of his actions during the killings. Only at the end of the questioning did the police discover he had received a gunshot wound in the left thigh which he had been keeping secret. He was consequently taken to Cooper Hospital for treatment. Charges were filed for thirteen counts of willful and malicious slaying with malice aforethought, and three counts of atrocious assault and battery. Ultimately, he was diagnosed with paranoid schizophrenia by psychologists, and found to be insane, making him invulnerable to criminal prosecution. When he was able to leave Cooper Hospital, Unruh was sent to the New Jersey Hospital for the Insane (now Trenton Psychiatric Hospital). Unruh's last public words, made during an interview with a psychologist, were, "I'd have killed a thousand if I had enough bullets." Unruh's is considered to be the first single event of mass murder in U.S. history. He died in 2009 after a lengthy illness at the age of eighty-eight. The incident became known as the Walk of Death.

Chapter 20: Michael Robert Ryan

On August 19th, 1987, Michael Robert Ryan, twenty-seven, shot and killed sixteen people, and wounded another fifteen, before killing himself, in Hungerford, Berkshire, England.

Michael Ryan was born on May 18th, 1960, to Alfred and Dorothy Ryan. He grew up in South View, Hungerford, where people remembered him as sullen and quiet. In school he was an underachiever and was never involved in social events or sports. After graduating, he attended college to become a building contractor, but soon dropped out and continued living with his parents. His mother would indulge him with anything he wanted: cars, insurance, gas, his first rifle. When Ryan was old enough, he purchased a shotgun and other weapons, which he proudly displayed in a glass cabinet in his bedroom. Ryan's guns gave him the feeling of power and control that he had always needed but lacked.

Ryan would brag to people about his false exploits, making himself out to be far more talented and experienced than he actually was. He told people that he had served in the Second Parachute Regiment of the British Armed Forces, that he was getting married, and that he owned a gun shop. He would become exceedingly annoyed if people did not believe him, and his mother would often corroborate these lies to people in a frantic effort to help her son feel better.

He was obsessed with the military and purchased army jackets, survival gear, and masks. He even convinced the police to permit him a license to own more powerful firearms. They were unable to refuse him as he had no record of psychological instability and no criminal record; however, they specified that Ryan install a suitable Chubb steel cabinet in which to safely lock his weapons. Ryan also subscribed to magazines on endurance skills and guns, including *Soldiers of Fortune*, and was an admirer of violent films such as *Rambo: First Blood*. In 1985, when Ryan was twenty-five, his father died of cancer. The loss affected him intensely and he became more and more inhibited, frequently going off alone to the shooting range, or working on cars by himself. It was during this time that he lost his caretaker job at a girls' school.

Just months before the massacre, Ryan joined the Tunnel Rifle and Pistol Club in Wiltshire. The manager later accounted that Ryan spent a lot of time at the club and that he was "a very good shot," showing unswerving accuracy over large distances.

On December 11th, 1986, Ryan was granted a firearms certificate which covered the ownership of two handguns. He later had the certificate amended to cover a third handgun in April of 1987. One month before the shooting, Ryan applied for another variance to cover two semi-automatic rifles, and that was approved on July 30th. At the time of the shooting spree, he was in possession of, and fully licensed to own, the following weapons:

- 1 x Zabala Shotgun

- 1 x Browning Shotgun

- 1 x Beretta 92FS 9mm Semi-automatic Handgun

- 1 x CZ ORSO .32 Caliber Semi-automatic Handgun

- 1 x Type 56 7.62x39mm Semi-automatic Rifle

- 1 x M1 Carbine .30 7.62x33mm Semi-automatic Rifle

On August 19th, 1987, in Hungerford, Berkshire, England, Michael Ryan, then twenty-seven, armed with his Beretta and both Semi-automatic rifles commenced his killing spree. At 12:30pm, Susan Godfrey, thirty-five, and her two little children, were approached by Ryan who told her to put the children in her car. He then took Susan into the nearby bushes and shot her fifteen times in the back. The Police arrived shortly after, but Ryan had already begun shooting at another location by that time.

He drove his silver Vauxhall Astra GTE to a gas station where he pumped gas and shot at the cashier, but missed her. He then entered the store and attempted to fire at her again at close range, but the magazine fell out from the Rifle; it's believed he inadvertently hit the release mechanism. He left the gas station and continued towards Hungerford.

At about 12:45pm, Ryan was seen at his home in South View, Hungerford. After loading his Vauxhall Astra with his weapons, Ryan attempted to leave, but the car would not start. Ryan fired five shots into the back of his Vauxhall. Neighbors reported seeing him frantically moving between the house and the car before he returned indoors and killed his mother, Dorothy, sixty-one, and the family dog.

Ryan then soaked his home with the fuel he had bought earlier in the day and set his house afire. The fire consequently destroyed three surrounding properties. He then removed the shotguns from the trunk of his car and went next door where he shot and killed husband and wife, Roland Mason, seventy, and Sheila Mason, sixty-nine, who were in their back garden. Sheila was shot once in the head and Roland six times in the back. Jack Gibbs, sixty-six, and his sixty-three year old invalid wife, Myrtle, were next to die.

On foot, Ryan roamed the streets firing at people. Marjorie Jackson was shot as she watched Ryan from the window of her living room, and fourteen year old Lisa Mildenhall was shot by Ryan in both legs as she stood outside her home. Mildenhall would recall that Ryan smiled at her before crouching and shooting. After pulling Dorothy Smith, seventy-seven, into her home, Marjorie Jackson telephoned George White, a colleague of her husband, Ivor Jackson. She informed Mr. White that she had been injured. Her husband insisted on returning home and George offered to drive him. On the trail towards the Common, Ryan encountered a family walking their dog. Upon seeing Ryan with his weapons, Kenneth Clements, fifty-one, raised his arms in a gesture of surrender as his family climbed over a wall and ran to safety. Ryan ignored the signal and killed Clements, who fell to the ground still clutching the leash of his dog.

Returning back to South View, Ryan fired twenty-three rounds at Officer Roger Brereton, who had just arrived at the scene in response to reports of gunfire. Brereton was hit four times and his car veered and crashed into a telephone pole. He died sitting in his patrol car, radioing to his colleagues that he had been shot. Ryan next turned his weapons on Linda Chapman and her teenage daughter, Alison, who had turned onto South View moments after Brereton was shot. Ryan fired eleven rounds from his semi-automatic into their Volvo 360; the bullets travelled through the bonnet of the car, hitting Alison in her right thigh. Ryan also shot through the windscreen, hitting Linda in the left shoulder. As Ryan reloaded his weapons, Linda reversed the car, exited South View, and drove to the local doctor's office, crashing into a tree outside the surgery. A bullet was found lodged at the base of Alison's spine. During an operation to remove it, surgeons decided that the risk of paralysis was too great, and the bullet was left in place.

Just after Linda and Alison Chapman had driven away, George White's Toyota drove towards Ryan, Ivor Jackson in the passenger seat. Ryan opened fire with his Type 56 Rifle, leaving White dead and Ivor Jackson brutally injured. White's Toyota crashed into the rear of Officer Brereton's Police Car. Ivor Jackson pretended to be dead and hoped that Ryan would not move in for a closer look.

Ryan continued on and came out on Fairview Road, killing Abdul Rahman Khan, eighty-four, who was mowing his lawn, and proceeded to shoot and injure his next door neighbour, Alan Lepetit. Ryan then shot at an ambulance which had just arrived, shattering the window and injuring emergency paramedic Hazel Haslett, but Haslett sped away before Ryan was able to fire at her again. A crowd had now gathered, and Ryan proceeded to fire at windows and shoot at people who appeared on the street. He then shot and wounded Mrs. Betty Tolladay who had stepped out of her house to rebuke Ryan; she had assumed Ryan had been shooting at paper targets in the woods.

The police were now informed about the happenstances in the neighborhood, but their evacuation plan was not fully successful. A police helicopter took off and followed Ryan's movements almost an hour after he set his home on fire, and was hindered by media helicopters and journalists responding to reports of the attacks. A single police officer managed to monitor Ryan and his artillery; he recommended that armed police be used as Ryan's armaments were beyond the capabilities of Hungerford Police Station's scant firearms locker. On Hungerford Common, Ryan went on to shoot and kill a young father of two, Francis Butler, twenty-six, as he walked his dog. He also shot at teenager Andrew Cadle, but missed the boy, allowing Cadle to speed away on his bicycle. Taxi- cab driver Marcus Barnard, thirty, slowed down his car as Ryan crossed in front of him. Michael shot him with the Type 56, causing massive damage to his head and killing him. Barnard had been detoured towards the Common by a police diversion as communication between ground forces and the police helicopter remained intermittent.

Ann Honeybone was wounded by a bullet as she drove down Priory Avenue. Ryan then shot at John Storms, an ambulance repairman, who was parked on Priory Avenue, hitting him in the face. Storms crouched below the dashboard of his vehicle; he heard Ryan fire twice more at his van and felt the vehicle shake, but he was not hit again. A local builder named Bob Barclay ran from his nearby house and dragged Storms out of his van and into the safety of his home.

Ryan then walked towards the town center of Hungerford where police were attempting to evacuate the public. During his walk, Ryan killed Douglas Wainwright, sixty-seven, and injured his wife, Kathleen, while they were in their car. Kathleen Wainwright would later say that her husband hit the brakes as soon as the windshield shattered. Ryan fired eight rounds into the Wainwright's vehicle, hitting Douglas in the head and Kathleen in the chest and hand. Mrs. Wainwright, seeing that her husband was dead, and that Ryan was approaching the car and reloading, unbuckled her seatbelt and ran from the car. The couple had been in town visiting their son, a policeman on the Hungerford force. Kevin Lance was next to be shot; he was hit in the upper arm as he drove his Ford Transit along Tarrant's Hill.

Further up Priory Avenue, handyman Eric Vardy, fifty-one, and his passenger, Steven Ball, drove into Ryan's path while travelling to a job in Vardy's Leyland Sherpa. Ball later recalled that he saw a young man, Kevin Lance, clutching his arm and running into a narrow side street. As

Mr. Ball focused on Lance, Ryan shattered the windshield with a burst of bullets. Eric Vardy was hit twice in the neck and upper torso and crashed his van into a wall. Mr. Vardy would later die of shock and hemorrhage from his neck wound. Steven Ball suffered no serious injuries. Throughout his movements, Ryan had also opened fire on a number of other people, some of whom were grazed or wounded. Many of these minor casualties were not counted in the eventual total.

At about 1:30pm, an hour after starting his shooting spree, Ryan crossed Orchard Park Close into Priory Road, firing a single round at a passing red Renault 5. This shot killed the twenty-two year old driver, Sandra Hill. A passing soldier, Carl Harries, rushed to Hill's car and attempted to apply first aid, but Sandra Hill died in his arms. After shooting Hill, Ryan continued to shoot his way into a house further down the Road, killing the occupants, Victor Gibbs, sixty-six, and his wheelchair-bound wife, Myrtle. Ryan also fired shots into neighboring houses from the Gibbs' house, injuring Michael Jennings and Mrs. Myra Geater.

Ryan moved on down Priory Road where he spotted Ian Playle, thirty-four, returning from a shopping trip with his wife and two young children. Playle crashed his car into a stationary car after being shot in the neck by Ryan; his wife and children were unhurt. Soldier Carl Harries again rushed over to administer first aid to Mr. Playle, but again the wound proved to be fatal. After shooting and injuring sixty-six year old, George Noon, while he was in his garden, Ryan broke into the John O' Gaunt Community Technology College, which was empty due to summer holidays. Ryan barricaded himself in a classroom where he once had been a student.

Police surrounded the building and negotiators made contact with Ryan only after he'd taken potshots at circling helicopters. At one point Ryan waved what seemed to be an unpinned grenade at them through the window, though reports differ as to whether Ryan really was armed as such. Police attempted to entice Ryan out of the school, but these attempts failed. At 6:52pm, Ryan committed suicide. One statement Ryan made towards the end of the negotiations was widely reported. He said, "Hungerford must be a bit of a mess. I wish I had stayed in bed." Hungerford is a small community. At the time of the shooting spree, it had a population of about 5500 citizens. It was policed by two sergeants and twelve constables, and on August 19th, 1987, the duty cover for the section consisted of one sergeant, two patrol constables and one station duty officer.

A number of factors hampered the police

response:

- The telephone exchange could not handle the number of 999 calls made by witnesses.

- The Thames Valley firearms squad were training forty miles away.

- The police helicopter was in for repair, though was eventually deployed.

- The local police station was undergoing renovations and only two phone lines were in operation at the time.

Chapter 21: Patrick Henry Sherrill

The term "Going Postal" was coined as a result of this killing spree. On August 20th, 1986, Patrick Henry Sherrill, a "disgruntled postal worker," killed fourteen fellow employees at the United States Post Office in Edmond, Oklahoma.

Sherrill was a recluse and socially incompetent. He was unable to hold a job for long and blamed management for his problems. His fascination with guns was fed by service in the U.S. Marines and active involvement in the Oklahoma Air National Guard, where he became a small arms expert. Aggravated at being officially disciplined by his postal supervisor on numerous occasions, Sherrill had, on two occasions, threatened retribution. After receiving a warning the day before, he reported to work on the morning of August 20th armed with three semi-automatic handguns and ammunition. He entered the facility, shot his Supervisor to death, and tracked his co-workers through the building, killing fourteen and wounding six. He then killed himself.

In 1987, a seven thousand page United States Postal Inspector's Report analyzed the Edmond massacre, and a one-day Congressional Hearing allowed the survivors and families a brief forum on March 18th, 1987. Each concluded that measures should have been in place to profile Sherrill and prevent his hiring, and to apply Occupational Health and Safety Standards and Federal regulations to Postal facilities.

No words can assess or mitigate the shooting's terrible impact on the victims and their families. Emotional and physical recovery was slow but sure. To honor the dead and the survivors, in 1989 the community of Edmond and the United States Postal Service placed a large sculptural memorial on the grounds of the Edmond Post Office. Sculptor Richard Muno depicted a standing man and woman holding a yellow ribbon; they are surrounded by fourteen fountains, one for each victim. The inscription lists the victims: Patricia Ann Chambers, Judy Stephens Denney, Richard C. Esser, Jr., Patricia A. Gabbard, Jonna Ruth Gragert, Patty Jean Husband, Betty Ann Jared, William F. Miller, Kenneth W. Morey, Leroy Orrin Phillips, Jerry

Ralph Pyle, Paul Michael Rockne, Thomas Wade Shader, Jr., Patti Lou Welch.

The Edmond incident was one of fifteen homicide incidents by postal employees from 1986 through 1999 in which thirty-four postal workers and six non-employees were killed. In turn, these spawned numerous workplace violence studies by Criminologists, Psychiatrists, and Federal Agencies. New hiring, employee management, and safety practices resulted, and federal law concerning homicide against Federal employees was expanded in 1996 (after the 1995 Oklahoma City Bombing) to include all Federal employees.

In perspective, by the year 2000, workplace violence took the lives of an average of one thousand people per year, in all workplace environments. Of those, only .2 percent of incidents involved postal workers. It is ironic and unfortunate that, at the end of the twentieth century, the Edmond Post Office Massacre was most often remembered for instigating the use of the term "going postal" to describe workplace violence in general.

The following is an excerpt from

Serial Killers Case Files Excerpt

Available in eBook, Paperback and Audiobook editions

Karla Homolka, the eldest of three daughters, was born on May 4th, 1970 in St. Catharines, Ontario, Canada, to Karel and Dorothy Homolka. Paul Bernardo was born on August 27th, 1964 in Toronto, Ontario, Canada, to Marilyn and Kenneth Bernardo. Paul and Karla met in 1987 and married in 1991. Shortly after they married, it was all downhill from there. Before they started their team rape and killings in 1991, Bernardo already had quite the history of rape, although he was not known to the authorities at that time. Between May 1987 and July 1990, he had raped eighteen young girls between the ages of fifteen and twenty-two.

His first murder victim was Tammy Homolka, Karla's younger sister. Bernardo encouraged Karla to drug her sister. When she did, Bernardo raped her before she woke up. Several months later they drugged Tammy again and both of them raped her, but this time Tammy died after choking on her own vomit. The police ruled it an accidental death, not knowing that before they called 911, Bernardo and Homolka had redressed Tammy and removed any incriminating evidence. Tammy Homolka died at the tender age of fifteen on December 23rd, 1990. Meet Leslie Mahaffy, a young girl, only fifteen, born on July 5th, 1976, and murdered on June 16th, 1991. Two day before her death, Leslie went out for an evening with a few friends. Her curfew was 10 p.m. as the Scarborough rapist was active and like many parents, Leslie's were afraid. Unfortunately, Leslie was having fun with the girls and ignored the ground rules set up by her parents. Her parents anticipated that she would break curfew and decided to teach her a lesson which they would forever regret. Leslie arrived home after 2 a.m. to find herself locked out of the house. She did not know what to do so she called a friend to see if she could stay over, but her friend's mom told her to go home and face the consequences.

Bernardo was crouched behind a car when Leslie came strolling by. Carrying a hunting knife, he forced her into his car and drove her to his house where he undressed her, blindfolded her, and videotaped her naked. He was going to have vaginal intercourse with Leslie but he ejaculated prematurely. When Karla woke up, he gave her instructions on how he wanted her to have sex with Leslie while he videotaped. This done, he instructed the submissive Karla to film him while he sodomized Leslie. The brute power of his anal penetration caused Leslie to cry hysterically. After twenty-four hours of disgusting rape and torture, the couple killed Leslie and, later that night, Bernardo used a circular saw to dismember her body and place her in cement.

On June 29th, 1991, a couple enjoying canoeing trip on Lake Gibson spotted a concrete block in the water. The cement block had what looked like animal flesh coming out of the cracks. There were anglers on the bank; they were asked to help retrieve the cement block. After splitting it with a crowbar, they were devastated when they saw a foot and the calf of a human crawling with maggots.

Enter Kristen French, born May 10th, 1976, a beautiful fifteen year old young girl. On April 16th, 1992, one month shy of her 16th birthday, she was walking home from school when Homolka lured her over to her car on the pretense of asking for directions. As Kristen was giving directions on the map, Bernardo, brandishing a knife, attacked her from behind and forced her into the car. This hostage-taking was observed by several witnesses. A BOLO was sent out to all units and a sketch was prepared of Bernardo by a witness. Kristen was kept for three days, being raped and tortured while the couple videotaped it all, and was forced to drink large quantities of alcohol before she was killed by Bernardo and Homolka. She was found in a ditch on April 30th, but as she was not dismembered, the investigators did not believe it was the same person who had killed Leslie Mahaffy.

The Green Ribbon Task Force was set up by the police with Superintendent Vincent Bevan taking the lead. The F.B.I. in the U.S. was consulted in an effort to profile the rapist. Citizens were concerned and kept their children at home. In the meantime, after the death of

Kristen French, the newlywed-killing-duet moved to the Niagara Falls area. As the drawing sketch of the rapist was plastered on TV, in post offices, in stores, and sidewalks, the police received calls saying that the man they were looking for resembled a man named Paul Bernardo. The investigators went to Bernardo's home where he claimed he was not the rapist/killer but admitted that, yes, the picture did resemble him, which he said was embarrassing. While the detectives were there, they noted that the car in the driveway looked nothing like the Capri which witnesses had seen, but instead was a Nissan. Paul Bernardo, therefore, was not considered a suspect. Police were no further ahead and Bernardo continued his spree of rape and murder of teenage girls. By February, 1993, Bernardo made a mistake that would put him in the limelight as a suspect. After he blackened both eyes of Homolka and knocked out several of her teeth, she called 911. The police in Niagara Falls took her to the hospital and began investigating the matter. Karla was admitted to hospital and her uncle came to visit her. She whispered to him that Bernardo had killed Leslie Mahaffy and Kristen French and went on to tell her uncle that he was indeed the Scarborough Rapist.

Author's Note: she never mentioned about the death of her sister Tammy. Homolka hired lawyer, George Walker, and told him that she wanted immunity if she gave up Bernardo. Walker said he would see what he could do.

The next day, on February 11th, 1993, Homolka's lawyer, George Walker, met with Director, Murray Segal, of the Crown Criminal Law Office. Walker told Segal that they had videotapes of the rapes, and Segal advised Walker that, considering Homolka's involvement in the crimes, full immunity was unlikely. Paul was arrested and charged with the murders of

Mahaffy and French and the rapes of several young girls. It was not until the 19th of February that police were granted a warrant to search Benardo's and Homolka's house. They did not, however, find any videotapes as Homolka had claimed. They did find a complete register in Bernardo's handwriting of all the murders and rapes, as well as books on serial killers, and perverted sex magazines. The much-wanted videotapes were in the possession of Bernardo's lawyer who surrendered them when he withdrew from the case. Before the tapes were handed to the police, a plea bargain was arranged based on Homolka's testimony. She would receive twelve years for each of the two victims (not her sister). The prosecutor said that it had to be done in order to nail Bernardo. Her earliest release date would be June, 2001.

Once the videotapes were obtained from Bernardo's lawyer, it clearly showed that

Homolka was heavily involved in cruel sex acts with both of the girls. Her lawyer could see for himself that she was a willing and eager participant in the crimes. As this news broke, public outrage for her plea bargain grew. The media dubbed it the worst deal the Canadian government had ever made with a criminal witness.

About The Author

RJ Parker

RJ was born and raised in Newfoundland and now resides in Ontario and Newfoundland, Canada. Parker started writing after becoming disabled with Anklyosing Spondylitis. He spent twenty-five years in various facets of Government and has two professional designations.

To date, RJ has donated over 1,900 autographed books to allied troops serving overseas and to our wounded warriors recovering in Naval and Army hospitals all over the world. He also donates a percentage of royalties to Victims of Violent Crimes.

If you are a police officer, firefighter, paramedic or serve in the military, active or retired, RJ gives his eBooks freely in appreciation for your service.

CONTACT INFORMATION

Facebook:
http://www.facebook.com/RJParkerPublishing
Email: Agent@RJParkerPublishing.com
Website: www.RJParkerPublishing.com

Twitter: @AuthorRJParker

Made in the USA
Coppell, TX
24 April 2021